P9-CKG-237

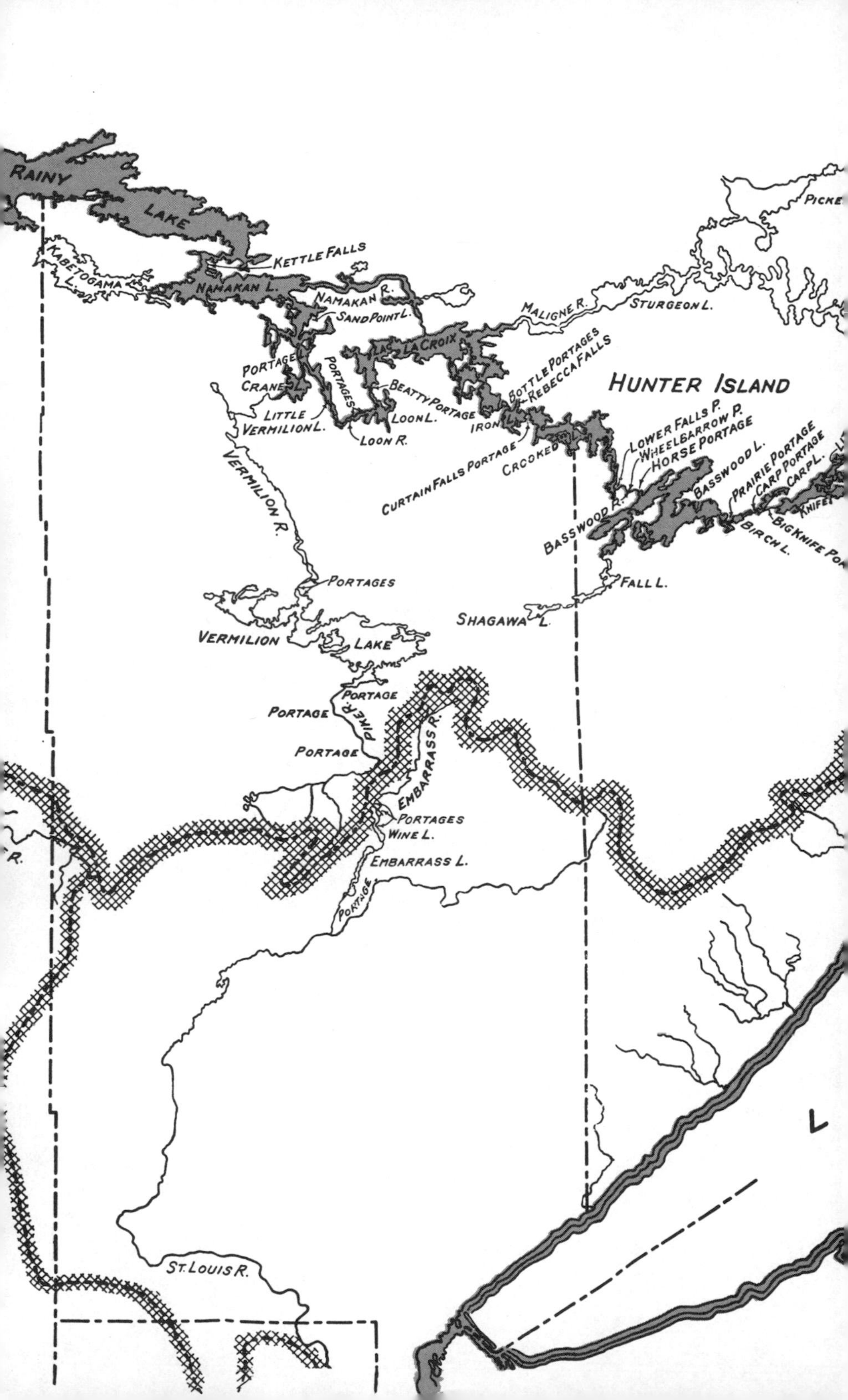

RAINY LAKE
KETTLE FALLS
KABETOGAMA L.
NAMAKAN L.
NAMAKAN R.
SAND POINT L.
MALIGNE R.
STURGEON L.
LAC LA CROIX
PORTAGE
CRANE L.
PORTAGES
BEATTY PORTAGE
LOON L.
LOON R.
LITTLE VERMILION L.
BOTTLE PORTAGES
REBECCA FALLS
IRON L.
HUNTER ISLAND
CURTAIN FALLS PORTAGE
CROOKED L.
LOWER FALLS P.
WHEELBARROW P.
HORSE PORTAGE
BASSWOOD L.
BASSWOOD R.
PRAIRIE PORTAGE
CARP PORTAGE
CARP L.
KNIFE
BIG KNIFE PO
BIRCH L.
VERMILION R.
PORTAGES
FALL L.
SHAGAWA L.
VERMILION LAKE
PORTAGE
PIKE R.
PORTAGE
PORTAGE
EMBARRASS R.
EMBARRASS
PORTAGES
WINE L.
EMBARRASS L.
PORTAGE
ST. LOUIS R.

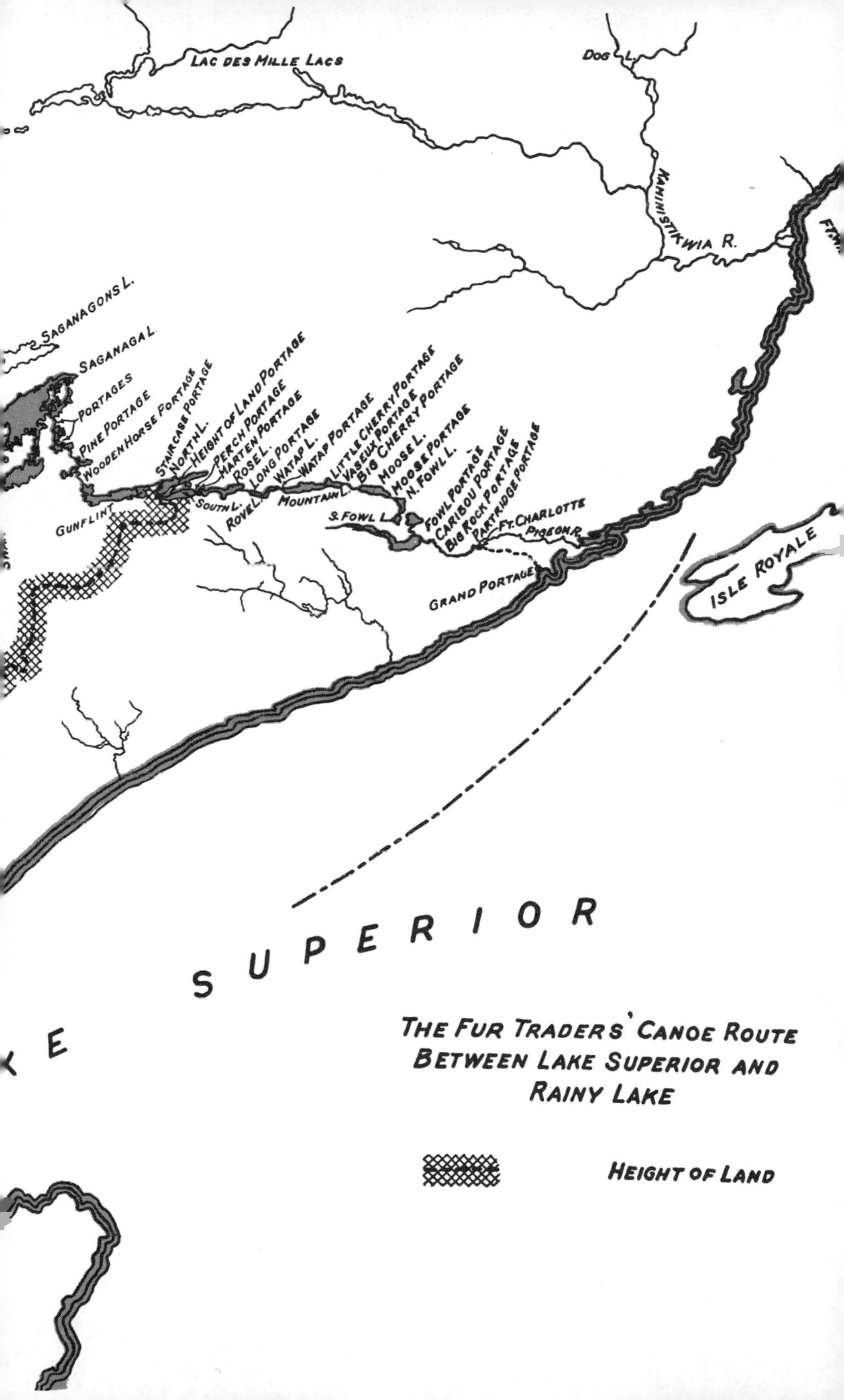

THE FUR TRADERS' CANOE ROUTE BETWEEN LAKE SUPERIOR AND RAINY LAKE

The Voyageur's Highway

The Voyageur's Highway

MINNESOTA'S BORDER LAKE LAND

by

Grace Lee Nute

THE MINNESOTA HISTORICAL SOCIETY
St. Paul

This volume is printed from the
SPECIAL PUBLICATIONS FUND
of the Minnesota Historical Society

INTERNATIONAL STANDARD BOOK NUMBER 0-87351-006-2

LIBRARY OF CONGRESS CATALOG CARD NUMBER: 65-63529

Manufactured in the United States of America

20 19 18 17 16 15 14 13 12 11

Publisher's Note

The Minnesota Historical Society *first published* The Voyageur's Highway *in 1941. Since then it has undergone ten additional printings for a total of thirty-eight thousand copies in print. It still attracts readers today and continues to serve as a dependable source of historical information. Thus the MHS Press is pleased to be reprinting the work again in 1988, with a newly designed cover, to keep it in print.*

Grace Lee Nute's reputation as a skilled historian and talented writer on the North Country is well deserved. On the pages that follow, the eras of the fur trade and voyageur come alive; the personalities of the iron rangers take shape; and loggers and their way of life are sharply etched. For the most part the information she imparts has stood the test of time. It is important, however, that modern readers keep in mind that the book is nearly a half century old, and it reflects the data and attitudes current in the 1930s.

Since that time, new works on the North Country have been published that add considerably to the bank of knowledge available. Since then, too, historians have become more sensitive in their treatment of Indian peoples and other minorities, being less likely to write of them only from the white people's point of view. In The Voyageur's Highway *readers will find an occasional phrase or word that will be jarring; no attempt has been made to change any part of the text to delete such usages. We ask, however, that readers make an effort to read more recent works—books that should be added to those in the bibliography at the end of this book. Some suggested reading includes other volumes published by the Minnesota Historical Society: Elden Johnson,* The Prehistoric Peoples of Minnesota *(rev. 3rd ed., 1988); Carolyn Gilman with essays by Alan R. Woolworth, Douglas A. Birk, and Bruce M. White,* Where Two Worlds Meet: The Great Lakes Fur Trade *(1982); Robert C. Wheeler, Walter A. Kenyon, Alan R. Woolworth, and Douglas A. Birk,* Voices from the Rapids: An Underwater Search for Fur Trade Artifacts, 1960-73 *(1975); William E. Lass,* Minnesota's Boundary with Canada: Its Evolution since 1783 *(1980); Marx Swanholm,* Lumbering in the Last of the White-Pine States *(1978); Edward W. Davis,* Pioneering with Taconite *(1964); David A. Walker,* Iron Frontier: The Discovery and Early Development of Minnesota's Three Ranges *(1979); R. Newell Searle,* Saving Quetico-Superior: A Land Set Apart *(1979).*

Foreword

THE MINNESOTA HISTORICAL SOCIETY *takes pleasure in publishing this volume. It has a history of its own. Frank Brookes Hubachek, a Chicago lawyer, for twenty-five years has spent much time in the Superior-Quetico region, roaming the country by canoe and snowshoe. Some years ago he bought a tract of virgin white pine in Minnesota's border-lakes country to save it from the ax. There he started a private project for reforestation and the conservation of other wilderness values, and his enthusiasm for the wild beauty and romantic past of the region increased. He was amazed to discover that few of the visitors to that region realized how far back in recorded American history its unique and colorful story begins. So Mr. Hubachek, a native Minnesotan, resolved to see what could be done to better the situation. He appealed to the Minnesota Historical Society for help and the result is the present volume.*

Mr. Hubachek's part in producing this book did not end with pointing out the need for it and getting Dr. Nute to write it, however. Without his substantial contributions in time, money, and enthusiasm, and his interest in the details of production, the volume would hardly have materialized. Such enlightened interest deserves abundantly the recognition accorded it in this foreword.

The author of this volume is well known as an authority

on the way of life of the voyageur, the indomitable, rollicking product of the fur trade, whose pathway almost inevitably led through the region described in the following pages. In 1934–35, as a fellow of the John Simon Guggenheim Foundation, she traced the life story of two famous explorers of America — Radisson and Des Groseilliers. Her right to tell the story of the border-lakes region is undeniable, her ability to do so well is unquestioned.

The actual printing of this book was made possible by the generosity of a member of the society, who wishes to remain anonymous. By the terms of the gift the proceeds from the sale of this book are to become the nucleus of a Special Publications Fund of the Minnesota Historical Society, which may be used only for the printing and publishing of such historical materials as do not fall within the province of the society's quarterly magazine or its other regular publications. The proceeds from the sale of all volumes published by means of the Special Publications Fund are to be used to augment the fund. It is the wish of the donor that others may follow his example by increasing the fund so that it will become a notable factor in bringing Minnesota's history to the people of the state.

ARTHUR J. LARSEN

MINNESOTA HISTORICAL SOCIETY
ST. PAUL

Acknowledgments

TO LIST *all who have aided in the preparation of this book would require considerable space, for it seems to have caught the imagination of many persons. All who came to my assistance in planning it, supplying data, recounting experiences in lumber camps, permitting the use of songs and translations, and paddling my canoe and portaging my pack along the voyageur's highway are offered my very sincere gratitude. A few deserve special thanks: first and foremost, Frank B. Hubachek, whose enthusiasm for the north woods is as contagious as his zeal for their preservation is untiring; various members of the staff of the Minnesota Historical Society, especially Mary Wheelhouse Berthel and Bertha L. Heilbron; Dr. Thomas S. Roberts, director of the Minnesota Museum of Natural History; Dr. George A. Thiel of the geology department of the University of Minnesota; Victor Johnston of the Minnesota Tourist Bureau; Robert O. Sweeny; Harrison Sletten; Charles Murray; Elizabeth Bachmann; Robert A. Beveridge; Ray Qualley; and my excellent guides, Joseph Kerntz and Frank Hrenn. The vignettes, the title page, and the cover design are the work of Jane McCarthy. The illustrations reproduced in the volume are accredited to their proper sources in the list of illustrations.*

GRACE LEE NUTE

MINNESOTA HISTORICAL SOCIETY
ST. PAUL

Contents

Illustrations

Illustrations

Illustrations

The North Country

The North Country is a siren. Who can resist her song of intricate and rich counterpoint – the soaring harmonies of bird melodies against an accompaniment of lapping waters, roaring cataracts, and the soft, sad overtones of pine boughs? She wears about her throat a necklace of pearls – Saganaga, La Croix, Basswood, and the other border lakes – strung on the international boundary line. Her flowing garments are forever green, the rich velvet verdure of pine needles. In autumn she pricks out the green background with embroidery of gold here and scarlet there. Winter adds a regal touch, with gleaming diamonds in her hair and ermine billowing from her shoulders. Those who have ever seen her in her beauty or listened to her vibrant melodies can never quite forget her nor lose the urge to return to her.

The North Country seems so young – and is so old. Many who paddle their canoes over Basswood Lake, portage at the Staircase, or pitch their tents at Curtain Falls, will be surprised to learn that these names, and most of the others used on the boundary, are centuries old, older by far than Minneapolis, Indiana, Missouri, and other regions and cities from which hundreds of visitors come to canoe on northern Minnesota lakes. The region was well known and its topographical features had famous names very early in American history. Over the waters of Gunflint, Saganaga, Basswood, and the other border lakes since the beginning of recorded American history has passed a succession of picturesque figures – Sioux, Cree, and Chippewa Indians; dashing French explorers; humble but vivacious voyageurs in gay sashes, singing *chansons* from medieval France; dour Scotsmen; scions of old English houses; canny Yankees; and men whose names are known throughout the world – the Sieur de la Vérendrye, Sir Alexander Mackenzie, Peter Pond, and David Thompson. No secluded backwaters were the boundary lakes, but part of a busy thoroughfare to empire, teeming with life and incident as long as the fur trade flourished.

The men who opened up this area made history and lived lives that still fascinate. Only a few of them can be discussed here, but readers who find an appeal in the knightly character of La Vérendrye, whose blood stirs on reading of Alexander Henry's perilous trips and John Tanner's years of Indian captivity in the border country, or who long to envision this region in its pristine beauty will find at the end of this book references to more detailed books and manuscripts. Peter Pond's quaint Yankee-ese amuses even in modern print, and David Thompson's matter-of-fact diaries and narrative are good companions for a winter's evening. Then take a book of voyageur songs and let some gifted friend play and sing them in French. Better still, let the accompaniment be the violin, as it was in picketed forts on Rainy, Vermilion, and Basswood lakes while voyageurs made merry on long winter evenings. Nowhere can one find folk songs of finer content and musical expression. The reader has not listened to *J'ai cueilli la belle rose*, if he doubts this.

Strangely enough, there is not much in print about the North Country in the modern period – since 1880. Two or three books on the iron ranges tell of the excitement of boom

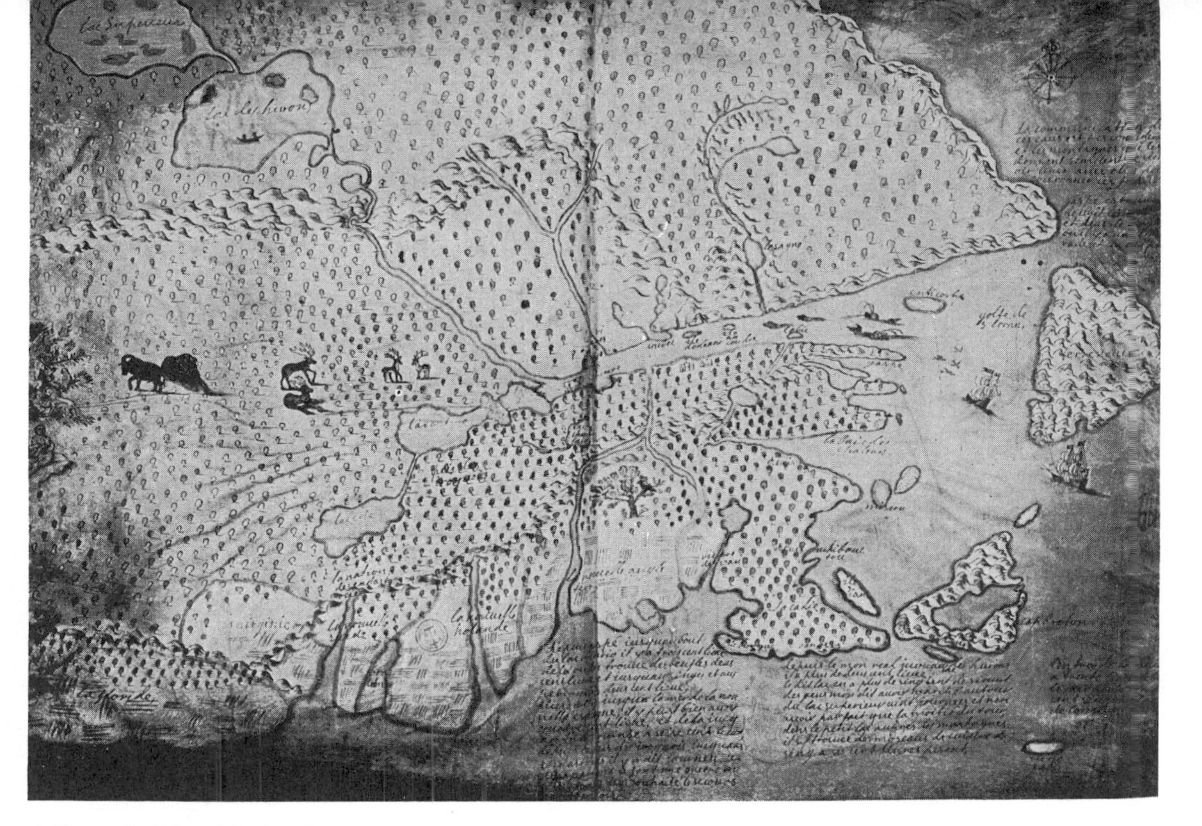

A French Map Made about 1658

It shows one of the earliest delineations of Lake Superior. In the legend is the following reference to that lake: "Some people have told me of having gone for twenty days about Lake Superior without having circumnavigated half of it."

A Sketch of the Fond du Lac Post of the American Fur Company, 1826

days, but very little is on record about the soft-spoken foreigners who came to people northeastern Minnesota and who have given such an old-world charm to farms and settlements among the birches and pines. For this later period one must glean largely from the memories of the living men and women who made it. Miners, lumberjacks, timber cruisers, surveyors, railroad men, half-breeds, guides, and trappers have fascinating stories to tell, if the inquirer is willing to eschew conversation himself, except for well-placed questions, and to ignore the inevitable Peerless, without which the Muse does not co-operate. These are men whose acquaintance is worth cultivating, and the wise visitor will draw them out and learn history in an inimitable way.

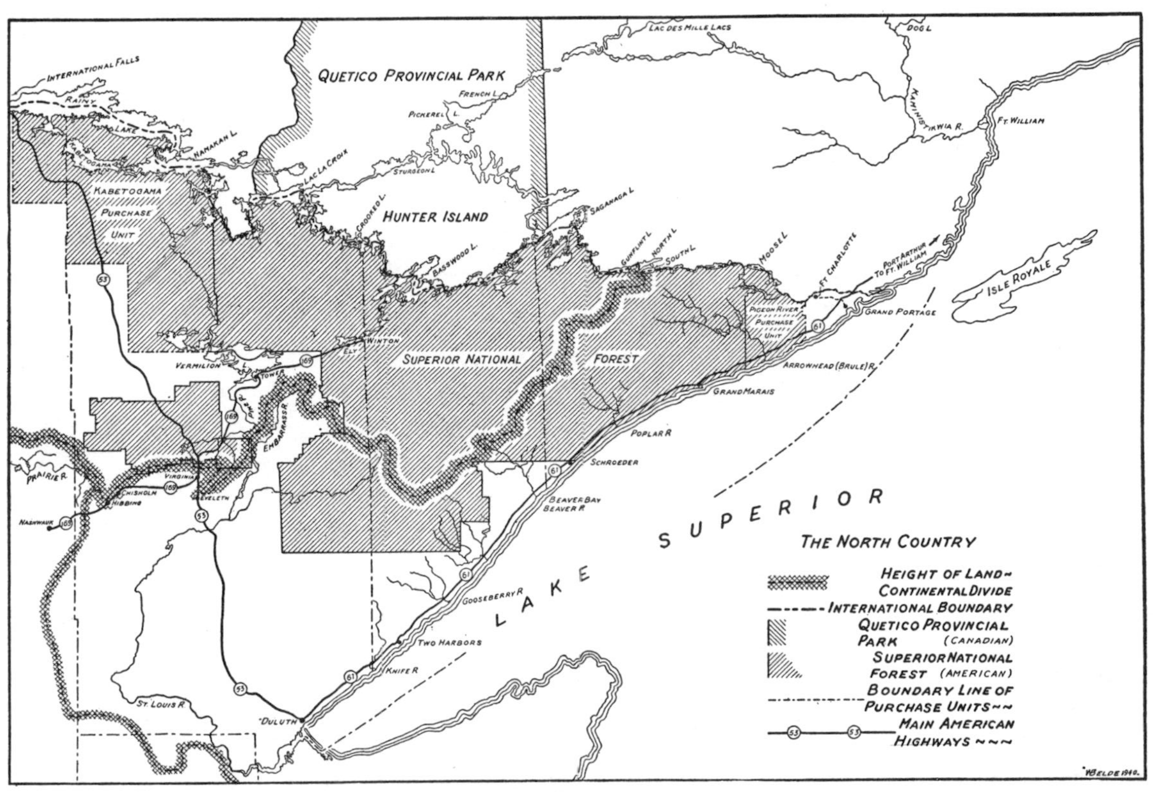

The North Country

Glimpses of the Past

The French Regime

Hardly were the Pilgrim fathers acquainted with their rocky fringe of continent when French explorers reached the very heart of North America. By 1660 both shores of Lake Superior had been visited and men had gone beyond—how far we do not know. On seventeenth century maps appeared a "Groseilliers River" on the north shore of Lake Superior. Whether or not this was the fascinating river now known as the Gooseberry is uncertain, but the name may well designate a stream visited by the Sieur des Groseilliers in the spring of 1660.[1] He seems to have explored at least a part of the north shore that spring in company with his young brother-in-law, Pierre Esprit Radisson, and they may have used one of the several Indian portage routes from Lake Superior to the Rainy Lake–Winnipeg River canoe route to the West. Some historians are inclined to the view that the Groseilliers River of the early maps was the Pigeon River of today and that the two brothers-in-law actually knew and used the famous Grand Portage at the mouth of Pigeon River.[2] Even if they did not venture inland toward Rainy Lake, it was only a short time

[1] "Groseilliers" is the French word for gooseberry bushes.

[2] Circumstantial proof of this contention is the fact that Alexander Henry, the Elder, in his account of his first trip up the river now known as the Pigeon, invariably refers to it as the Groseilliers River, though his spelling of the French word leaves something to be desired. See page 23, below.

before a Frenchman *did* explore that ancient canoe route along Minnesota's present northern boundary.

The first Frenchman actually known to have ventured from Lake Superior over the canoe route toward Rainy Lake was a resident of Three Rivers in the province of Quebec, which was a prolific nursery of explorers and voyageurs. His name was Jacques de Noyon and early documents refer to him as a "voyageur," a term that soon came to have a special meaning. In ordinary French it means merely "traveler," but in North America it meant a canoeman in the fur trade. There are several references to De Noyon in French records, but one in particular, written in 1716, refers to him as having wintered "about twenty-eight years ago" in the Rainy Lake country on the "Ouchichiq River." This was probably an early name for Rainy River, since it is mentioned as leading to "the Lake of the Assiniboin [*presumably Lake Winnipeg*] and from there to the Western Sea." A document of 1717 states that "some voyageurs have already been clear to the Lake of the Assiniboin."

After the 1680's the French records are silent about the region for thirty years or so, though it is almost certain that other white men penetrated the area west of Grand Portage during those years. Then, in the years after 1731, the boundary waters were the usual thoroughfare to a West that became better and better known as the years rolled by. Explorers and fur traders found routes, built forts, established practices and customs, and gave names to physical features. It was in 1731 that Pierre Gaultier, whose title was Sieur de la Vérendrye, began his explorations beyond Grand Portage; and it was about 1760 that the last French post was abandoned in the *pays d'en haut* — the "upper country" — as the traders called this region and other parts of the West of that day. So the

French regime may be said to have lasted just a century in this borderland

THE BRITISH REGIME

With 1760 came the conquest of Canada by the British. France lost its fine, great colony in 1763. English and British colonial explorers and traders now became common on the border waters. Though on paper a large part of Minnesota passed to Spain in 1763, and though the Americans between 1776 and 1783 fought and won a war with Great Britain, this border area remained practically British till the close of the War of 1812. Kings came and went, governments rose and fell, wars were fought, and boundary lines were placed at will, but the border country cared little. Its life went on as before, full of activity, danger, adventure, the struggle for existence, the round of ordinary daily life in a region that was virtually a law unto itself.

The period after the Revolutionary War witnessed the interplay of three great trading companies in the region: the Hudson's Bay Company, the North West Company, and the American Fur Company. It was also the heyday of the voyageur, that dauntless mariner of the western waters. Over the lakes and streams of the north woods floated his light bark canoe propelled by red, flashing blades to the tune of his Loire Valley *chansons.*

About the year 1768 John Askin cleared the site of Grand Portage, at the Lake Superior end of the border-lakes canoe route, to make ready for a post there. From that time till shortly after 1800 Grand Portage was the great inland depot of the North West Company's fur trade. Other companies and individuals also made it the center of their operations. Every July a great gathering of traders and voyageurs was held there, to which men came from far out on the Great

Plains, from the Oregon country, and from bleak tundras beneath the Arctic Circle. A large part of the trade of a vast hinterland, embracing the center of the continent and many of its fringes, passed through this narrow channel on its way to the great fur marts of Europe and Asia.

Another post was established at Rainy Lake. To it the men from Athabaska, hundreds of miles to the northwest, could travel and return in one season; but if they went on to Grand Portage, they might find western lakes and rivers blocked with ice on the return trip. So an Athabaska House was a prominent feature of the Rainy Lake post. A special set of canoemen from Grand Portage met the Athabaska men there, received their packs, and gave them their annual supplies in return.

Most of the border-lake posts were dependent on one of these two forts. Even the Lake of the Woods posts were, as a rule, only wintering houses from the Rainy Lake fort. There were few forts, moreover, that did not lie along the boundary waters. Red Lake, Leech Lake, and Vermilion Lake had posts; the country between them and the border waters had few, if any.

The North West Company had things pretty much its own way on the border till 1793, when the Hudson's Bay Company, long quiescent along the shore of Hudson Bay till stung into action by its rival, began to establish posts at Rainy Lake and on Rainy River. Competition flared, particularly from 1793 to 1798 and again from 1818 to 1821. Between 1798 and 1804 the North West Company's chief rival here was an offshoot of itself, generally called the X Y Company. After the War of 1812, and particularly after 1823, Americans of John Jacob Astor's American Fur Company were the principal competitors, with posts at Grand Portage, Grand Marais, Vermilion Lake, Moose Lake, Basswood Lake, Rainy Lake, Rainy River, Warroad, Roseau Lake, and Lake of the Woods. So keen did the competition become that finally in 1833 the Hudson's Bay Company, which had absorbed the North West Company in 1821, bought off the Yankee traders with an annual payment of three hundred pounds sterling. The Hudson's Bay Company posts were practically the only ones on the border lakes between 1833 and 1847. This company had few posts south of the border at any time, except in the valley of the Red River of the North and on one or two of its affluents. Even these were short lived. When Minnesotans speak of old Hudson's Bay Company posts on Minnesota soil, they almost invariably have in mind forts of the North West Company or of the American Fur Company.

The American Regime

The Yankees who followed close on the heels of the British traders and explorers witnessed many boundary disputes between the United States and Great Britain in the twenties, thirties, and forties of the last century, while the first infant settlements were burgeoning into life in the region that in 1849 was to be named Minnesota. Attempts to settle these disputes were made again and again, by treaties, conventions, boundary surveys and commissions, arbitration by foreign princes, and other expedients, till in 1842 the Webster-Ashburton Treaty laid the basis for a lasting peace, the settlement of the boundary dispute, and many years of close friendship between the United States and Canada.

Geologists became the next explorers of the region, particularly between 1848 and 1880. A false gold boom, begun by one of them, led to a temporary opening of this frontier to settlement at the close of the Civil War; but it was really the discovery of iron ore that brought permanent settlers to the region in the eighties and early nineties. From the villages of the Vermilion and Mesabi ranges, which were founded at the time of the mining booms, men from Finland and southeastern Europe gradually slipped out into the wilderness, cleared little farms, and began a very independent sort of existence. Their culture has become a unique part of Minnesota's life.

The logging boom then came upon the region early in the twentieth century, when lumberjacks by thousands cut the great pines in winter and often labored as harvest hands in the Red River Valley and on Dakota prairies, or on whalebacks and other ore boats on the Great Lakes, in summer. These red-shirted, stag-trousered, calked-booted men were close rivals of the voyageurs in romance and hard, dangerous living.

The monarchs of the forest fell. Americans began to see the loss they had sustained in the deforestation of most of the North Country. Just as the first World War broke in Europe, a conservation program was initiated in Minnesota to preserve its remaining forests, lakes, streams, wild animals, flowers, birds, and wilderness.

A Fallen Monarch

Aerial View from Upper Basswood Falls and United States Point, Basswood Lake
The international boundary line has been inserted.

Mountain Lake

A Camp on Cypress Lake

Boundary Routes and Disputes

FROM La Vérendrye's explorations in 1731 until shortly after the beginning of the Seven Years' War in 1756 French fur traders came and went over the boundary waters between Lake Superior and Lake of the Woods. Two routes were in use in the eastern part of this water highway: the Pigeon River route from Grand Portage, over the present boundary waters to Lac La Croix, and thence to Rainy Lake; and the Kaministikwia River way, which passed from the mouth of that stream, where Fort William now is, to Lac des Mille Lacs, by portages to Pickerel Lake, through Sturgeon Lake, down the Maligne River, and into Lac La Croix, where it joined the first route. After English traders penetrated the region in the 1760's, the old French route via the Kaministikwia was practically forgotten. It was rediscovered, almost by chance, by Roderick Mackenzie in 1798. It became the usual route after 1803 when the North West Company, fearing the imposition of custom duties by the American government, made Fort William its central depot in place of Grand Portage. The northern canoe route remained the first section of the customary highway to the West thereafter until 1821. The Hudson's Bay Company's absorption of the North West Company in that year made it possible for all traders to use the cheaper route through Hudson Bay, which earlier had been closed to all save Hudson's Bay Company men. However, there was a trickle of traffic over the Kaministikwia route for many years after 1821, especially after the Canadian government sent Simon J. Dawson and Henry Y. Hind over it on an exploring trip in 1857 and 1858.

Between these two converging canoe routes lies an area of considerable size and forest wealth in Canada, a southern part of which is usually referred to as Hunter Island. It is an island only in the sense that waterways of lakes and rivers practically set it off from other land. Long ago Americans began to claim that this island belonged to the United States, and occasionally the claim is still set forth in newspapers. David Thompson referred to "Jonathan's" avarice in this matter when he was surveying the boundary waters in 1823 and 1824. Probably a variant of the Grand Portage route passing to the north of the island was in fairly common use at one time and another, but it was never the usual route from Grand Portage to Rainy Lake. The criterion for the frontier line in the long boundary dispute between England and the United States after the treaty of 1783 was "the customary waterway." All territory south of such a waterway was to be American; all north of it, British.

Despite several attempts, France and England had not been able to fix on a boundary line between New France and the British colonies when Great Britain acquired Canada by the Treaty of Paris in 1763. East of the Mississippi the boundary did not matter much from 1763 to 1783 because the entire region was British. West of the Mississippi the boundary presented no problem, for Louisiana had been ceded to Spain in 1763 and, since Spanish colonists never pressed far enough to the north to come into serious conflict with British colonials, no boundary line between Canada and Spanish Louisiana was ever agreed upon. When the United States purchased Louisi-

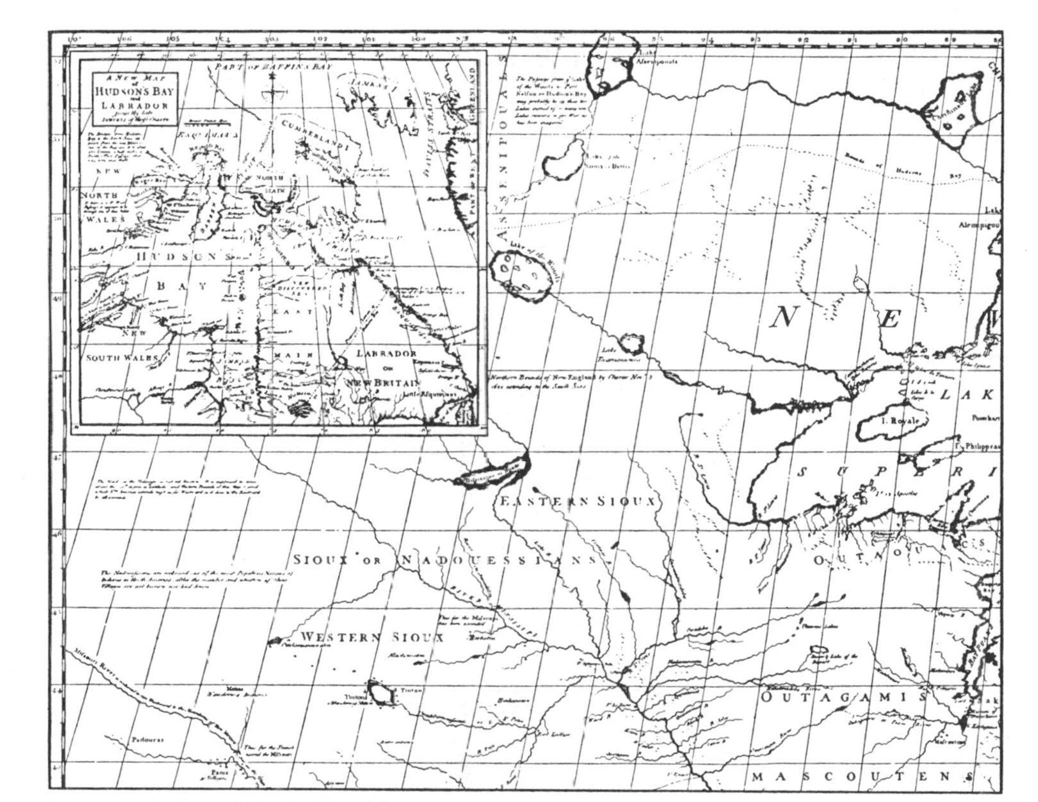

Part of John Mitchell's Map of 1755

ana in 1803, however, it was obvious to everyone that some settlement of the boundary question would have to be made in the near future. Americans were not like Spanish colonials. The Yankees were ever on the move. As early as the winter of 1805–06 an American military expedition under Zebulon Montgomery Pike visited the headwaters of the Mississippi. Anything could be expected from such enterprising people.

The treaty which ended the War of the Revolution was believed at first to have settled the boundary question to a point a little west of Lake of the Woods. The treaty stipulated that the boundary line should run through Lake Superior northwest of Isle Royale to "the Long Lake," presumably Pigeon River, and through the water communication between it and the Lake of the Woods; "thence through the said lake to the most northwestern point thereof, and from thence, on a due west course, to the River Mississippi."

Although it was not then realized, this boundary line was impossible. Mitchell's map of North America, published in 1755 and herein reproduced in part, was the reason for the confusion in the minds of the commissioners, who relied upon it for the slight knowledge they had of the region beyond Grand Portage. It shows "Long Lake" as a broad estuary at the mouth of an unnamed river emptying into Lake Superior about thirty miles southwest of the mouth of the Kaministikwia River; and it depicts the Mississippi apparently as rising a little northwest of Lake of the Woods. The course of the river near its source is covered by an inset map, but the larger map includes a statement that the Mississippi is supposed to rise in latitude 50°, that is, north of the present international boundary.

Very soon the fur traders let it be known that the proposed boundary line was an impossibility. A line run due west from any point on Lake of the Woods would never intercept the Mississippi, which actually rises near latitude 47°. As everyone in Great Britain and Canada appears to have believed that it was absolutely necessary that British traders should have access to the upper Mississippi, attempts were begun shortly to run the boundary anew, and in such a way as to strike the river.

About 1790 an effort was made by the British to run a long finger of British territory down as far as the Falls of St. Anthony, but Jefferson succeeded in thwarting that plan. In 1794, the time of Jay's Treaty, two remedies were proposed: a boundary line from the present site of Duluth to Red Lake River and the Mississippi — an impossible line; and a boundary line from the mouth of the St. Croix River below the Falls of St. Anthony to the old canoe route between Grand Portage and Rainy Lake. How narrowly the United States missed all right to the eastern border lakes may be understood if it is recalled that Jay yielded practically every other point to the British negotiators.

Fortunately for dwellers on the Mesabi and Vermilion iron ranges, not to mention other Americans who profit from the natural resources in the wedge of territory now generally called the Arrowhead Country, Jay did not accept this line. A joint boundary survey was then proposed. This was never carried out. In 1802 a line north from the source of the Mississippi to the northwesternmost point of the Lake of the Woods was all but accepted by the King-Hawkesbury convention. The timely intervention of the Louisiana Purchase by the United States halted these negotiations midway.

After the War of 1812 the convention of 1818 between the United States and Great Britain settled the boundary line west of the Lake of the Woods and provided for a joint survey along the line of the old canoe route in the region lying between Lake Superior and the Lake of the Woods. Commissioners were chosen by each nation. In 1822, 1823, and 1824 these men were in the field exploring. All the commissioners omitted the Grand Portage route in their claims. The American commissioners claimed that the old French route from the mouth of the Kaministikwia River was the customary one; it, of the three routes, would give the United States the most territory. The St. Louis River route passing up that river and down the Pike through Vermilion Lake to Portage Lake was claimed by the British as the usual canoe route; it, of all the routes, would give them most territory. The British commissioners surveyed along the way that passed through Basswood Lake, as well as on the St. Louis River route, and some others; the Americans explored along the old French way and some of the other routes, though exactly which ones we do not know. Among the British commissioners was David Thompson, the famous trader and map maker, whose career is given in more detail later.

Until 1803 Thompson and other traders had continued to use the Grand Portage route. In that year the more northerly trail to the new fort, soon to be named Fort William, was followed by all but the X Y Company's men. This short-lived offshoot and rival of the North West Company coalesced with the "Big Company" in 1804, but some traders continued to use the Grand Portage route until 1806. The North West Company, to prevent a rival from competing, then sent men ahead of the competitor's brigade to cut down trees and otherwise obstruct the way. For some years after 1806, therefore, the old Grand Portage route was not in use.

By 1823 the Grand Portage route must have been clear again, for the commissioners passed that way surveying the boundary waters. It is interesting to note that Thompson told one of the other British commissioners that the new route from Fort William was much inferior to the old one in every respect and that the "*voyageurs* had to be coaxed and bribed into the use of it" when the change was made.

Though the commissioners reported in 1827 on their findings, they could not agree concerning article 7 of the treaty, which involved the identity of "Long Lake." So the boundary dispute remained unsettled. Finally, by the Webster-Ashburton Treaty of 1842, the long-drawn-out altercation was settled amicably. The Pigeon River route was chosen as the "customary waterway" and made the international boundary line.

The exact wording of the essential part of article 2 of the treaty is as follows: ". . . to the mouth of Pigeon River, and up the said river, to and through the north and south Fowl Lakes, to the lakes of the height of land between Lake Superior and the Lake of the Woods; thence, along the water communication to Lake Saisaginaga, and through that lake; thence, to and through Cypress Lake, Lac du Bois Blanc [*Basswood Lake*], Lac la Croix, Little Vermillion Lake, and Lake Namecan and through the several smaller lakes, straits, or streams, connecting the lakes here mentioned, to that point in Lac la Pluie, or Rainy Lake, at the Chaudière Falls, from which the commissioners traced the line to the most northwestern point of the Lake of the Woods. . . . It being understood that all the water communications and all the usual portages along the line from Lake Superior to the Lake of the Woods, and also Grand Portage, from the shore of Lake Superior to the Pigeon River, as now actually used, shall be free and open to the use of the citizens and subjects of both countries." Not the least strange part of this strange story is the fact that the treaty thus provides that both British subjects and Americans may use not only the waterway, but also the portages on the route.

The actual survey of the region to carry out the provisions of the treaty waited till the twentieth century for accomplishment. By the treaty of 1908 between Great Britain and the United States, a commission was established which located and monumented the line. Most of the field work was carried on between 1912 and 1918, although it was not finished till 1926. An exhaustive report was published in 1931.

The boundary questions between Canada and the United States seem definitely settled. Besides the commissions provided by treaty between the United States and Great Britain in 1908 and 1925, there is now a permanent body, the International Joint Commission, which has jurisdiction over all cases involving boundary waters or rivers crossing the boundary. It investigates matters referred to it by either country, and it may settle any matter of any nature that the governments of the two countries may agree to refer to it. It was created by treaty in 1909. Its successful functioning should be a revelation to a warring world, showing how neighbors can act and have acted for more than a quarter of a century.

Portaging between Jasper and Alpine Lakes

The East Half of Rebecca Falls

With Paddle and Packsack on the Quetico

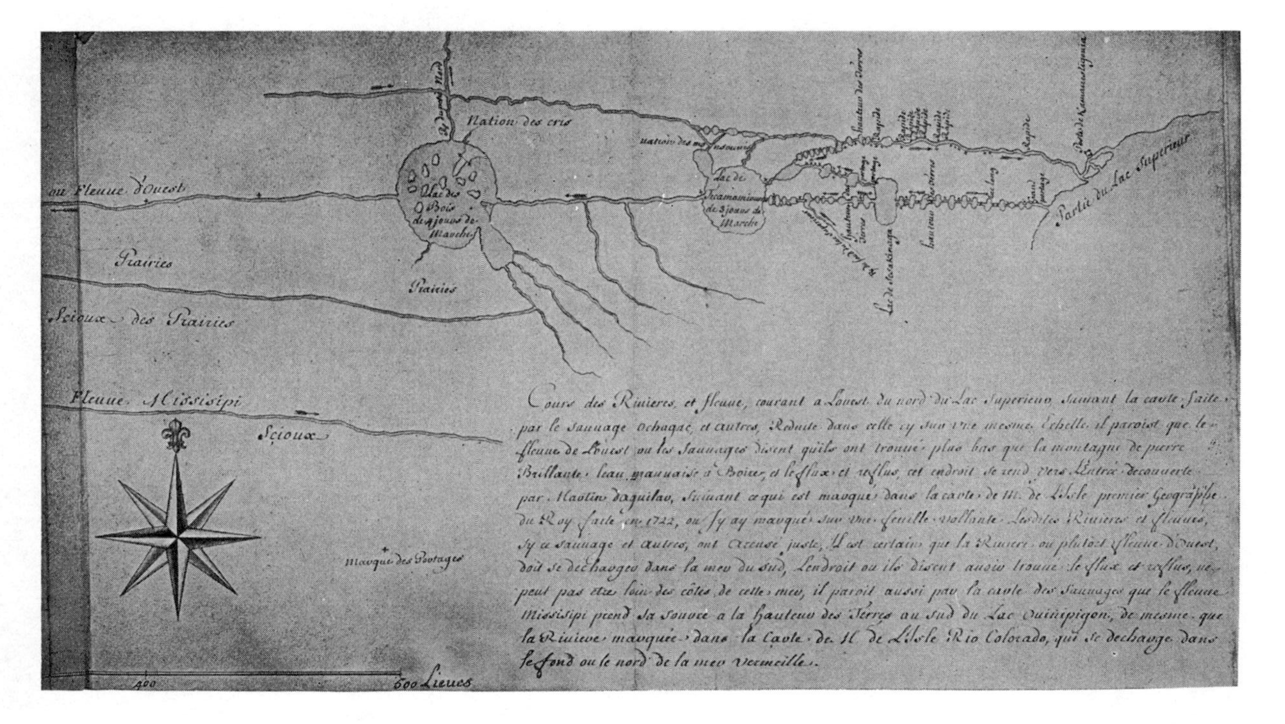

Auchagah's Map of the "Westward Flowing Rivers North of Lake Superior"

See page 21.

Famous Men of the Border

IT WOULD be unfair to the reader to omit personalities in this sketch of yesteryear on the border lakes. Nowhere did leadership, courage, and resourcefulness count for more than in "darkest North America." It is difficult to comprehend today what was involved in making a canoe journey from Lake Superior to Lake Winnipeg, especially before the days of numerous travelers in the heyday of the great fur companies. Besides the ever-present danger from Indians, there were unknown rapids and waterfalls. Food had to be carried by the traveler, who was journeying fast and could not stop to hunt and fish. There were no maps; the knowledge of islands and headlands that voyageurs carried in their heads was relied upon to get brigades of canoes though tortuous channels and between myriads of islands. Illness often overtook leaders or their men. Great storms took their toll of lives. And the mere toil of weeks and months of canoe paddling and freight portaging was enough to deter all but the strongest and most resolute of men.

Only the most famous of the great men of the fur trade can be mentioned here. It must not be forgotten, however, that for every one of these there were scores of less illustrious men, any one of whom could have told many a tale of adventure and incident.

The Voyageur's Highway

Pierre Gaultier, Sieur de la Vérendrye

In 1716 and 1717 France was trying desperately to find a substitute for its former route into the heart of the continent. From the 1650's to 1713 the best way was considered to lie through Hudson Bay, out of which a river or sea inlet was thought to lead to the Northwest Passage. Explorers went west and northwest in search of that elusive passage, but when Hudson Bay was turned over to the English by the Treaty of Utrecht in 1713, the "passage" had yet to be found. In order to continue the search and to maintain the fur trade with the far western Indians, a new French canoe route, which did not lie through British-held Hudson Bay, would have to be opened. So, from 1713 to 1731, attempts were made to find a substitute way. A post was established on Lake Pepin on the upper Mississippi in 1727 to prevent the Sioux from warring on the Cree and their western neighbors, the Assiniboin Indians. Only then could posts be established and a route opened via Rainy Lake, Lake Winnipeg, and the Saskatchewan and Assiniboine rivers.

By 1731 an explorer from Three Rivers, the Sieur de la Vérendrye, was en route to Grand Portage to find the Sea of the West. In his veins ran the blood of early Canadian explorers. Nevertheless, he had fought for France on the continent against the great Marlborough and had been left for dead at the battle of Malplaquet in 1709 when he was twenty-four years old. With him in 1731 went three of his sons, a nephew, and some forty-five men. Later a fourth son joined him. His nephew and a small body of men passed over the canoe route from Grand Portage to Rainy Lake late in the year 1731. Before winter set in, Fort St. Pierre had been established at the outlet of Rainy Lake. A fort remained there, almost without break, from that time till about 1900, when it was discontinued.

Thus more than two hundred years ago the Grand Portage canoe route began to be used by brigades of trading canoes. Picture to yourself the scene as these men caught their first view of pine-edged lakes in such numbers as they could scarcely have believed possible; as they toiled up the steps of the Staircase Portage; as they ventured cautiously down the treacherous waters of Basswood River; and as they saw the beauties of Lac La Croix unroll before their birch-bark prows. These were the first of thousands of white men whose feet were to pack down the soil of portage paths so firmly that the trails to this day are clearly visible in otherwise trackless wilderness.

In the spring of 1732 the remainder of La Vérendrye's party followed the advance guard to Rainy Lake and then went on to build Fort St. Charles on Lake of the Woods. Other posts followed – on Lake Winnipeg, on the Red River of the North, and out along the Saskatchewan River route to the Sea of the West. Other Frenchmen were soon in the West. Trading posts were built between Rainy Lake and Lake Superior – on Little Vermilion, Basswood, Saganaga, and Moose lakes. English explorers of the latter part of the century, when British traders were replacing French, wrote of these French posts as they learned about them from abandoned sites, the Indians, and other sources. Of the post on Saganaga Lake, Alexander Henry wrote in 1775: "This was the hithermost post in the north west, established by the French." And of the posts on Basswood Lake, Alexander Mackenzie wrote a few years later: "When the French were in possession of this country, they had several trading establishments on the islands and banks of this lake."

La Vérendrye got an Indian, Auchagah, to draw a map of the Rainy Lake region to guide him as he ventured into the unknown wilderness. Fortunately contemporary copies of it have been preserved in Paris — the first map in a long series of such documents prepared by French explorers and traders for the country between Lake Superior and Lake of the Woods. In the reproduction printed herewith, it is easy to distinguish some of the larger "vertebrae" of the spinelike column which the boundary lakes became in this unskilled cartographer's hands. For example, the source of the St. Louis River is shown, though it is called by its original French name, Fond du Lac River. Since one of the branches of the St. Louis River connects by a short portage with Namakan Lake, we may orient ourselves fairly readily in using this map.

Another early French map shows a post on "Vermilion Lake," which is our Little Vermilion Lake. This lake was on one of the war roads of the Sioux. Both the fort's establishment in 1736 by René Bourassa and its history for a few years are told in La Vérendrye's numerous and detailed reports to his superiors.

La Vérendrye, his sons, and his men remained in the West for many years, exploring rivers, lakes, and even the Great Plains in the hope of finding a way to the Sea of the West. They passed and repassed through the border lakes on their way to and from Montreal and elsewhere. It was on a border lake that La Vérendrye's son, Jean Baptiste, nineteen voyageurs, and the Jesuit missionary Aulneau were massacred by Sioux who had evaded the policing force on Lake Pepin. The grim tragedy is recorded in the name of Massacre Island in Lake of the Woods. It is of interest to note here that the names of many of the men in La Vérendrye's trading exploits are known through "engagements," or trading contracts, which every trader had to secure before leaving Canada for the *pays d'en haut*. Some of them have a familiar ring: Jacques La

Vallée, Paul Chevalier, François Provanché, Joseph de Laurier, Antoine Millet, and Jean Baptiste Renaud.

Alexander Henry, the Elder

One of the first Englishmen to go into the West after the conquest of Canada was Alexander Henry, usually called the Elder, a native of the colony of New Jersey. His nephew of the same name was also a trader in the Canadian West some years later. If the aroma of adventure clings to La Vérendrye's career before he ventured into the far West, how much more does it attach to Henry's narrow escape from death when the fort at Mackinac was taken by treachery of Indians in 1763. Henry was in the fort and was saved by the loyalty of an Indian woman who hid him in a garret. Though the Indians searched the attic, they did not find the hidden man, and he was one of the few white men who remained alive after the butchery.

In 1775 Henry passed along the border-lakes route to the far West. On the eighth of July, he ascended the "Groseilles," as he termed the Pigeon River, to the Partridge Portage, "where the river falls down a precipice of the height of a hundred feet." Next day, at Fowl Portage, he left the "Groseilles," and carrying canoes and merchandise for three miles, over a mountain, he and his companions came at length to a small lake. This was "the beginning of a chain of lakes, extending for fifteen leagues, and separated by carrying-places of from half a mile to three miles in length." At the end of this chain, he reached "the heads of small streams which flow to the northwestward." "The region of the lakes is called the Hauteur de Terre, or *Land's Height*," he writes. "It is an elevated tract of country, not inclining in any direction, and diversified on its surface with small hills. The wood is abundant;

but consists principally in birch, pine, spruce-fir and a small quantity of maple."

"By the twelfth," he continues, "we arrived where the streams were large enough to float the canoes, with their lading, though the men walked in the water, pushing them along." Next day he found the streams navigable, though interrupted by frequent falls and carrying places. On the twentieth he reached Saganaga Lake, "distant sixty leagues from the Grand Portage." "This," he explains, "was the hithermost post in the north-west, established by the French; and there was formerly a large village of Chipeways here, now destroyed by the Nadowessies [*Sioux*]. I found only three lodges filled with poor, dirty and almost naked inhabitants, of whom I bought fish and wild rice, which latter they had in great abundance. When populous, this village used to be troublesome to the traders, obstructing their voyages, and extorting liquor and other articles." He describes Saganaga Lake as eight leagues in length by four in breadth. "The lands," he continues, "which are every where covered with spruce, are hilly on the south-west; but, on the north-east more level." His men were by this time almost exhausted with fatigue, but, fortunately, the "chief part of the labour" was past.

Alexander Mackenzie

A traveler with early knowledge of the border waters was Alexander Mackenzie, later Sir Alexander Mackenzie. He was one of the leading traders, first in the North West Company and then in the X Y Company. He is remembered today chiefly for having discovered the Mackenzie River and for having been the first person to cross the North American continent in its northern latitudes. He has left many descriptions of the border lakes and their surroundings. Of Basswood

Lake, for example, he writes: "Then follows the lake of that name, but I think improperly so called, as the natives name it the Lac Passeau Minac Sagaigan, or lake of Dry Berries. . . . This lake is irregular in its form, and its utmost extent from East to West is fifteen miles; a point of land, called Point au Pin, jutting into it, divides it in two parts: it then makes a second angle at the West end, to the lesser Portage de Bois Blanc, two hundred paces in length."[1] Basswood River's channel he describes as "not wide" and as intercepted by several rapids in the course of a mile before reaching the end of today's Horse Portage, "over which the canoe and lading is again carried four hundred paces." He then mentions "very dangerous rapids, for two miles Westerly," before reaching the next portage, "which is two hundred and eighty paces." This is now Wheelbarrow Portage. Finally, a mile beyond, came the portage into Crooked Lake, eighty paces in length, which "is followed by an embarkation on that lake, which takes its name from its figure. It extends eighteen miles, in a meandering form."

He then describes the Picture Rock on Crooked Lake, a landmark today: "Within three miles of the last Portage is a remarkable rock, with a smooth face, but split and cracked in different parts, which hang over the water. Into one of its horizontal chasms a great number of arrows have been shot, which is said to have been done by a war party of the Nadowasis or Sieux, who had done much mischief in this country, and left these weapons as a warning to the Chebois [*Chip-*

[1] The portage is now called Horse Portage. It introduces the canoeist to Basswood River. In Mackenzie's day there were two portages, of two hundred and four hundred paces, respectively, and an intervening stretch of navigable water, which are now superseded by one long portage – Horse Portage. David Thompson gave the name of the second part of our Horse Portage as "Big Pine Portage"; and he refers to our Wheelbarrow Portage as "Little Stone Portage."

pewa] or natives, that, notwithstanding its lakes, rivers, and rocks, it was not inaccessible to their enemies."

There are many stories to account for the arrows in the rock. One of them tells how the Indians used the rifts in the cliff as a test of marksmanship. Archers in tipsy bark canoes in the moving waters below would try to place their arrows in cracks in the rock's face. Another accounts for the arrows by telling of a battle here between the Sioux and the Chippewa. David Thompson dates the reputed visit of the Sioux at about 1730. Still another story explains the arrows by describing a custom of the Chippewa, which required their young men to prove their skill by shooting arrows into the cracks of the cliff.

David Thompson

The man who knew the boundary country best in trading days was doubtless David Thompson. As a poor lad in London he showed such intellectual promise that he was given an education in a great charity school, and then went out to serve an apprenticeship with the Hudson's Bay Company in western North America. After fourteen years of service he left that company in 1797 and made his way eastward to Grand Portage, the inland headquarters of its powerful rival, the North West Company. As he passed on his way he kept a diary, the first of many of his that tell of the famous canoe route along Minnesota's northern boundary. He passed Bottle Portage, between Lac La Croix and Iron Lake, on July 18. He describes it as about three hundred yards in length and "uneven." That day he encountered canoes of traders from the Saskatchewan River and "2 Canoes of the Red River People." He "very near upset" in a "strong Current" just before reaching the portage at Curtain Falls, which he describes as about two hundred yards in length on the right-hand side of his

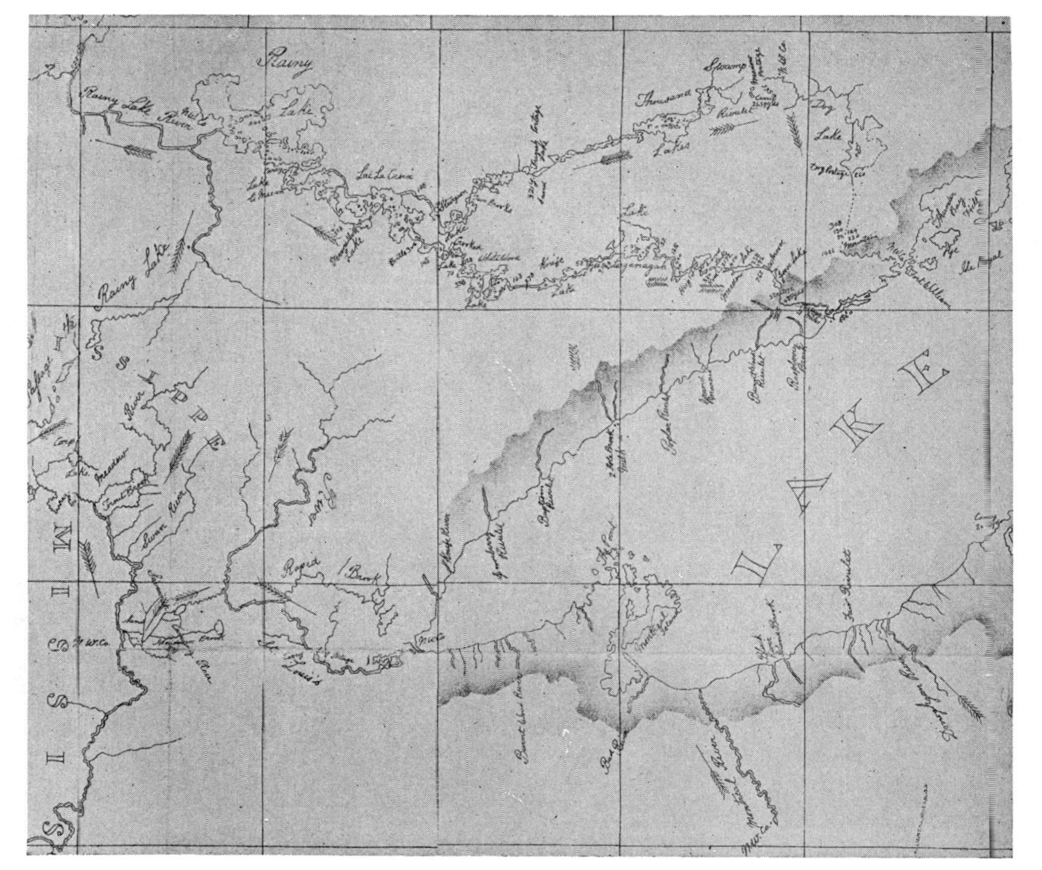

Part of David Thompson's Map, 1813–14

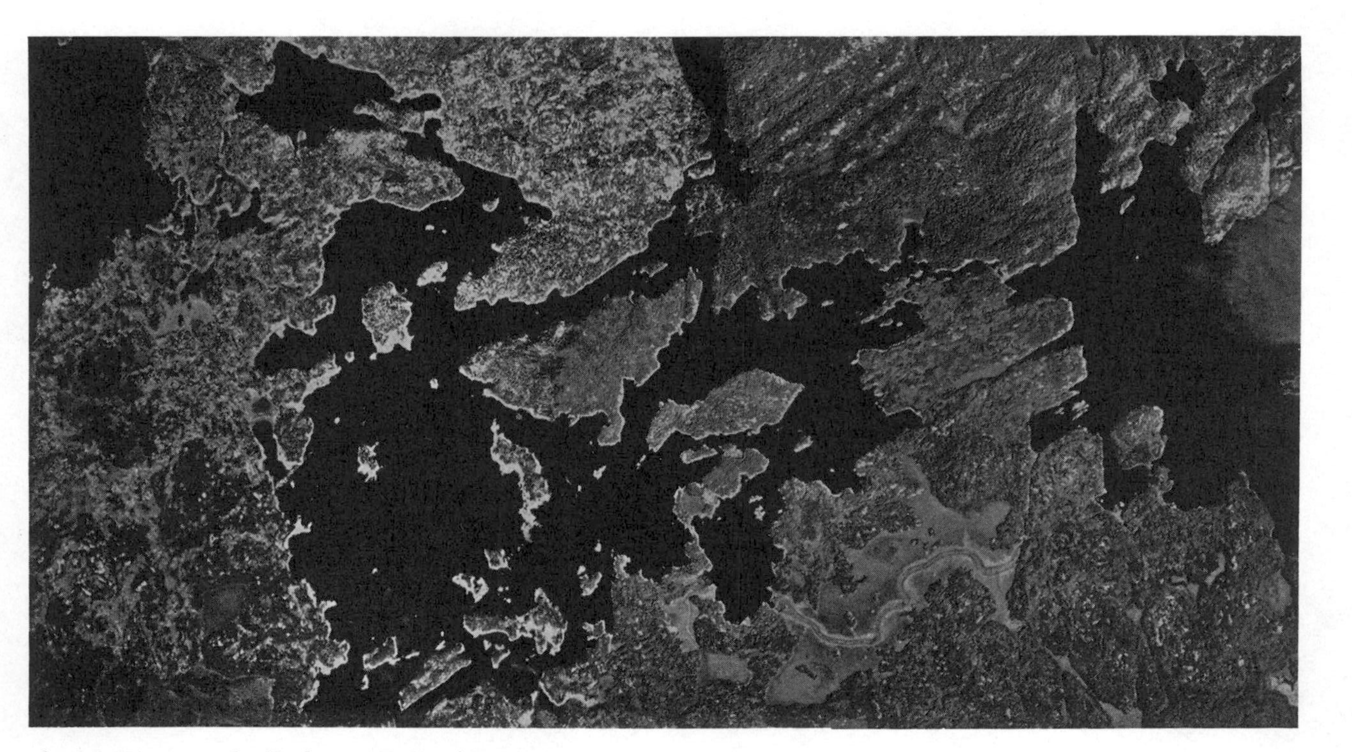

Aerial View of the Rebecca Falls Area

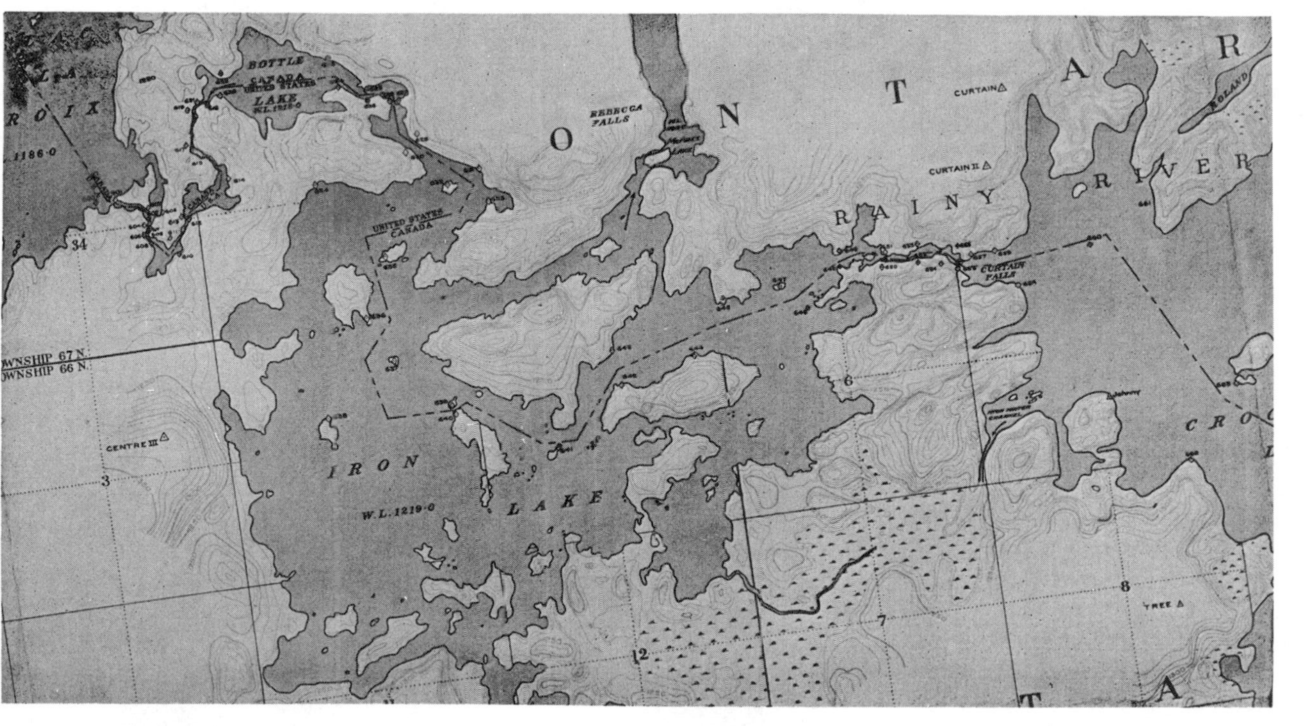

The International Joint Commission's Map of the Rebecca Falls Area

Curtain Falls

route. The unloading was "very bad" and the bank was steep. He gives the height of the falls as twenty feet. At nine thirty he and his people encamped for the night.

The next day he passed through Crooked Lake and up Basswood River, where he describes a "100 yds rapid," a portage "on the right," and then another portage on the right of about two hundred and fifty yards, and finally he emerged in Basswood Lake. There he made scientific observations and proceeded on his way to the "Soties House Fall & Portage with Canoe Build^{g}." This confusing reference is to a Saulteur, or Chippewa Indian, whose "house," or wigwam, was at the east end of Basswood Lake near the present Prairie Portage, where he was building a canoe.[2] The portage was 350 yards long and "rocky."

Thompson arrived at Grand Portage on July 22, five days from Bottle Portage. Modern canoeists who know the route are almost incredulous of this feat of fast paddling and portaging. On August 9, 1797, he was off again for the West, to Swan River. On August 11 he passed Goose (Fowl), Moose, Big Cherry, and Vaseux portages, and camped at Little Cherry Portage with "plenty of Musketoes." Next day at "Little New Portage" he "met 4 Canoes of Montreal Men" with the "Slave Lake Packs," who told the news that "the Day before they left the Rainy Lake 4 Souties Men killed each other in a drunken Quarrel." At "Big New Portage" he found several canoes of men camped for the night. Thompson got his goods across the portage that night. He was off at six thirty the next morning, August 13, passed Rose Lake and Perch Portage, where breakfast was eaten, and came to Height of Land Portage. During the day he went through Gunflint Lake to a portage where four canoes of men lay encamped. Thomp-

[2] The early French name for the Chippewa was "Saulteurs," or people of Sault Ste. Marie, their residence when the French first encountered them.

son joined them. Next day he went through Saganaga Lake, passed the canoe of "Monsr Chaboiellez," and put up for the night with four canoes of men. Next day he came up with Jonathan Cameron, a *bourgeois* or partner of the company; and Messrs. Grant, McKay, and Mackenzie overtook him. On to Knife Lake, where he passed some Indians – drunk. That night Cameron and two other North West Company men were in his encampment. Early on August 16 he passed Big Knife Portage and reached Prairie Portage, which he called "Great White Wood Portage." He found "4 Sotie & their families with . . . the meat of 2 moose dried – the House burnt to the Ground." Heavy rain came on and the white men encamped there, quite a party of North West men. Next morning at five fifty they were off in the rain on "White Wood Lake" (Basswood Lake) where he "saw the first Gull." Today the gulls still nest in June on tiny islands in the lake, the females brooding the eggs in the full blaze of the noonday sun without so much as a bush to shield them.

Thompson got to the falls in a "mizzling Rain." He gives the length of this portage at Upper Basswood Falls as 138 yards and locates it on the left side of the stream. "We then walked down along shore to the large Pine C[arrying] P[lace] of 338 yards," he writes; "met 6 Sotee Men & their Families – took Breakfast – at 1 PM set off . . . down the River . . . run 2 Rapids," crossed the "little Stone C[arrying] P[lace] on the right 128 y^{ds} good" and came to another portage on the left at Lower Basswood Falls – "its length 76 y^{ds} steep smooth Rocks on the lower side. The Fall ab[ou]t 13 feet perpend[icular] in 2 Ridges." Next he came to "Arrows stick^{g} in a Rock on the left," which, of course, was the Picture Rock on Crooked Lake.

The "grand Galles," apparently gravel bars in Crooked

Lake, are next mentioned, near "Mill Stone Rock" [*Table Rock*], and at 6:30 P.M., he "put up at a smooth Rock . . . with mizzling Rain." He "Killed 1 Duck" that day, apparently at the encampment. Early next day he was at Curtain Falls, where he and his men "were near upset" on their "Passage out." He notes "many Flocks of wild Pigeons flyg past." Passenger pigeons were not extinct then and passed in great flocks of many thousands over Minnesota's woods. On August 19 between Namakan Lake and Kettle Falls Thompson records that he "Killed 2 Pigeons." The following day he entered Rainy Lake.

The next year Thompson went back over another route and as far east as Sault Ste. Marie. On June 1, 1798, he left the Sault, reached Grand Portage "Thank God" on June 7 in time to watch brigade after brigade of canoes arrive from the West. These he lists in detail in his diary: "Monsr Le Tory . . . with 19 Packs of 78 @ 80 lbs weight"; "Monsr Frederique & the Lake Winepeg Island Portage & Rainy Lake Packs"; "4 Canoes of Mr Ogilvie's"; "Mr Sayer from Fond du Lac"; "Monsr [Jean] Baptiste Cadotte"; "Montreal Canoes"; "Mr Wm Thorburn" and "Mr Wm McGillivray"; "Mr Duncan McGillivray . . . with a wound in his leg—so bad as to render him unable to walk"; "Messrs McDonnel, Hughes, Chaboillez, McIntosh Richards & Felco"; "Mr Todd from lower Fort de Prairie" on the Saskatchewan; "Mr Roderic McKenzie"; "a light Canoe from Montreal . . . with Letters"; "Mr Cuthbert Grant, McLeod—McTavish & James McKenzie"; and the sailing vessel, the "Otter," from Sault Ste. Marie. All these and many more arrived between June 8 and 30. Grand Portage vibrated with events and personalities all that month, before it settled down once more to the quiet that characterized it for ten months of the year.

The Voyageur's Highway

Early in July Thompson set off again for the interior. The festivities at Grand Portage had obviously unsettled him a little, for he lost a whole month out of his reckoning. All his succeeding diary entries are just a month too early; for example, all the July entries are dated June. He breakfasted on July 18 on the Height of Land; "put up" that night at Cedar Rapids, "where we stopped & pitched the Canoe last year"; was on Saganaga and Knife lakes on the nineteenth; "passed 7 Portages or 8" on the twentieth; and spent that night in Crooked Lake, "a fine night but could not Observe for the woods." The next night he slept at the end of "Lake Mecan," now known as Namakan Lake.

Thompson continued with the North West Company for many years, most of which were spent in the far West – even as far as the Oregon country. Everywhere he kept careful diaries, all of which contain minute records of his course, mile by mile, in cartographer's terms, with accompanying maps. His is one of the sturdiest figures whose representation has come down to us from the fur-trade period. No one doubted his entire integrity; Indians, voyageurs, clerks, *bourgeois*, all knew that he would not traffic in liquor, that he would not cheat the Indians, that he would not put false entries in his books, and that Sunday morning he expected his voyageurs to assemble about him while he read the Scriptures to them. Picture to yourself a short, compact man, with black hair worn long about his head and cut square, a deeply bronzed complexion, and a short nose – in fact, the perfect double of John Bunyan, as all who knew him felt – sitting upon some shingle bank of Crooked Lake while he read to his men, "in most extraordinarily pronounced French, three chapters out of the Old Testament, and as many out of the New, adding such explanations as seemed to him suitable."[3] Though his men were Catholics and he was a Protestant, and though his pronunciation must have left some confusion in their simple minds, they listened both attentively and with utmost respect and were not known ever to have made a joke about the extraordinary performance, so great was their admiration for the man.

Thompson returned to civilization in 1812, taking his half-breed wife with him to his home in the province of Quebec. Soon he was asked to prepare a map of the country in which the North West Company had trading posts. This map hung for years in the board room at Fort William, the successor of the Grand Portage post. It is now in the possession of the province of Ontario. It bears Thompson's title: ". . . Map made for the North West Company in 1813 and 1814. . . . Embraces the Region lying between 45 and 60 degrees North Latitude and 84 and 124 degrees West Longitude comprising the Surveys and Discoveries of 20 years . . . by David Thompson Astronomer and Surveyor." Its scale is remarkable: fifteen miles to the inch. Joseph B. Tyrrell, who has published so much on Thompson, writes thus in the preface to his *Thompson's Narrative:* "Between the years 1883 and 1898, while engaged on the staff of the Geological Survey of Canada, it fell to my lot to carry on explorations in canoes, on horseback, or on foot, over many of the routes which had been surveyed and explored by David Thompson a century before. . . . Everywhere his work was found to be of the very highest order, considering the means and facilities at his disposal, and as my knowledge of his achievements widened, my admiration for this fur-trading geographer increased."

[3] These are the words of Dr. John J. Bigsby, who accompanied Thompson on a later expedition.

No one was so well qualified as Thompson to be the cartographer of the British part of the international commission set up after the peace of 1814 to determine the boundary line between the United States and Canada. So in 1816 he set forth once more, and for ten years he served in that capacity. In 1822 he was back at Grand Portage, by that time a forsaken spot with no hint of its former bustle and prestige. The next summer he spent with the commission mapping the old trade route from Grand Portage to Lake of the Woods, which was to be the boundary line eventually by agreement of the two nations. His maps and notes of the entire region are preserved in Toronto. They show that he was on Basswood Lake on July 8 and 9, 1823. His maps reveal that the old canoe route entered Inlet Bay from Birch Lake by way of the present Prairie Portage, went southwest of the large island in Inlet Bay, through the narrows into Bayley Bay, south of Norway Point, between some islands just northwest of Rice Bay, then north of the large island just east of Ottawa, or Ranger, Island, between Canadian Point and Ottawa Island, up through the narrows around United States Point, and down the Basswood River to Crooked Lake. It is interesting to note that in Thompson's day United States Point was called "Cypress Point." The "cypress" tree of past generations on the border seems to be today's cedar.

Thompson's maps end the controversy as to the site of the Hudson's Bay Company's post on Basswood Lake about 1825. Modern maps show it on Ottawa Island, close to the present ranger's post. In 1823, when Thompson passed, it was on a small cape on the north side of the narrows between Bayley Bay and Inlet Bay. Some thirty or forty years later the post may have been moved; at least there are evidences of a fort of about such an age not far from the present ranger's station.

Famous Men of the Border

Alexander Henry, the Younger

Alexander Henry, a nephew of the more famous explorer-trader of the same name, left a series of diaries of his trading activities about the year 1800 which have been published and which include detailed accounts of his trips on the border waters. In that year he reached Birch Lake on July 26, just a week after leaving Grand Portage. With his companions he crossed Birch Lake the same day and made the Big Basswood Portage, now called Prairie Portage, "near 300 paces long." On this portage the party met three canoefuls of men with packs eastbound from the distant Athabaska country. On one of the "Pine Islands" of Henry's day, which are impossible to identify now among the scores of islands in this lake, camp was made. The Indians here were making birch-bark canoes, and as Henry was in need of a new craft, he decided to pause while one was made for him. It may be mentioned that he also found the Indians on Saganaga Lake, Lac La Croix, and Namakan Lake making canoes.

Henry had to wait longer than he anticipated. The weather was hot and sultry and he whiled away the time getting blueberries from the Indian women and noting the trade canoes that passed. Roderick Mackenzie, among others, sped past in a light, or unloaded canoe, bound for Grand Portage, which he expected to reach in two days! Because of the heat the Indians refused to work on the canoe. Henry got angry and threatened them "with a good beating." Finally his own men had to finish the craft and Henry started off next morning at ten o'clock. For the canoe he paid sixty beaver skins or their equivalent in trade credits. His diary goes on to mention a portage (part of modern Horse Portage) on the Basswood River, followed by "several ugly rapids," and "Portage de la Pointe des Bois" (now Wheelbarrow Portage), over which his men "carried about 300 paces." The party then proceeded to Lower Basswood Falls, where there was "a portage of about 100 paces over a rock" to Crooked Lake. "At the Rock in Arrows," or Picture Rock, Henry "met nine canoes loaded with Athabasca packs." At sunset he got to Curtain Falls, where he stopped for the night.

Henry himself had one canoe in a brigade, as a flotilla of canoes was termed in those days. Besides the canoes already mentioned, he refers to meeting and passing many more. It is clear that the border lakes were busy places, at least in the summer months, a hundred and forty years ago.

Henry was back at Grand Portage in the summer of 1801, but he has left no account of that visit. The next time he went to the rendezvous, he left his old route at "Pointe du Mai," or Lob Pine Point, in Lac La Croix at the south side of the entrance to Martin's Bay, and passed up the Maligne River. He got to the new post, Fort William, which was still in process of construction, on July 3, 1803, and left again for his post on the Red River of the North on July 29. He remained in that area till 1808. From 1808 to 1811 he was in charge of three different Saskatchewan posts. In 1813 he was on the Columbia River, where he was drowned in 1814.

Dr. John J. Bigsby

A man who was neither an explorer nor a trader, but who traveled with David Thompson along Minnesota's border waters and drew our first authentic pictures of them was Dr. John J. Bigsby. He was the artist physician who was appointed the secretary of the British section of the boundary commission under the provisions of the Convention of 1818 between Great Britain and the United States.

He writes as he begins his tour in 1823: "The country be-

The Picture Rock, Crooked Lake

Portaging

Islands in Basswood Lake

On the long island Alexander Henry may well have had his canoe built. See page 33.

Bigsby's Sketch of Upper Basswood Falls, 1823

See page 36.

Bigsby's Sketch of Lac La Croix, 1823

tween Lake Superior and the Lake of the Woods is, like the whole watershed between Hudson's Bay and the Valley of the St. Lawrence, a rugged assemblage of hills, with lakes, rivers, and morasses, of all sizes and shapes, in their intervals. . . . They all communicate practically with each other, either by water or by portages, so that the traveller may reach the Lake of the Woods by many routes, differing only in danger, labour, and directness. Thus nineteen of the rivers which enter into Lake Superior west of the Grand Portage rise near Lake Boisblanc [*Basswood Lake*], the tenth lake on our route. All these are used from time to time by the Indians to get to Lake Lapluie [*Rainy Lake*], &c., and so is a chain of lakes leading westward from the Nipigon country to Lake Boisblanc."

Of the falls at Prairie Portage he writes: "A succession of rapids, closely shrouded in foliage, sometimes violent (and an expanse, sometimes called Carp Lake), bring us into Boisblanc Lake." He describes Basswood Lake with enthusiasm: "Its many islands, high and well-wooded shores, with pretty beaches of yellow sand, render it very picturesque. We passed a wintering-post of the Hudson's Bay Company, consisting of two or three comfortable huts on a cape." The lake, he notes, "is very crooked, and resembles the letter Z in shape."

Bigsby then recounts an incident that occurred on the return journey through Basswood Lake in the autumn: "We espied a canoe rounding a point to enter one of its [*the lake's*] deep bays. Being then very short of provisions we hastened after it, and found it in company with four others, all filled with Indians. They could only sell us some strips of dried deer's flesh, each a yard long and four or five inches broad. It looked like thick, red leather; but our men were glad of it to thicken their soup. While this purchase was going on, the gentle breeze drove a canoe full of women alongside mine. As we rocked on the wave, the women fixed their eyes with wonderment upon me sewing on a button. The needle having an eye, and carrying the thread along with it, caused many a low, soft note of surprise; but when I presented a needle and some thread to each of the dark ladies, they were delighted. Although their prattle was unintelligible to me, not so their thankful eyes."

On Basswood River the party encountered a "series of violent rapids and cascades, from three to five miles long . . . with their portages." Bigsby made a sketch of one of these cascades, Upper Basswood Falls, which is here reproduced. "At the lower end of one of these rapids," Bigsby continues, "there is an interesting relic of ancient Indian warfare in a hollow pile of stones, five feet broad by six long. It is now only three feet high, and has an aperture in the side, by which the rapids below may be watched. Each stone of the ground-tier (granite and gneiss) would require the united strength of three or four men to move it. Under this shelter in days now gone by, the Chippewas, or Wood Indians, used to watch for their invaders, the Sioux of the plains, – a race of horsemen and warriors living principally on buffalo."

The canoes "next came to a narrow of still water, the entrance in fact of Lake Croche . . . [*Crooked Lake*], about twenty miles long. This narrow is walled in by high precipices of shattered granite, beautifully striped downwards by broad bands of white, yellow, red, green, and black stains (vegetable). Until lately the arrows shot by the Sioux, during a conflict at this spot, might be seen, sticking in the clefts of the rocks." Bigsby is describing the Picture Rock, but like all the other early recorders he does not mention the vermilion drawings of animals on the flat face of the cliff just above the water line. Yet they are almost certainly genuine Indian drawings. Their age may be inferred from the fact that they represent practically all the animals of the region, including some now nearly extinct.

Bigsby's description of Lac La Croix reveals his manifold interests and his versatility: "The Lake of the Cross is thirty-four miles long by eighteen wide. . . . According to our survey, it contains 260 islands, often pine-tufted with rushy sides, besides rocks innumerable. Its shores are extremely capricious in their outlines, and often bare and high. The Indians have names for most of the localities, but we could seldom procure them." On the south shore of the lake he found wild rice growing "so abundantly and fine . . . that we sometimes could hardly push our canoes through it." The water-lilies he described as "superb, much the finest I have seen. They are about the size of a dahlia, for which they might be taken. They are double throughout, every row of petals diminishing by degrees, and passing gradually from the purest white to the highest lemon-colour. There is in the neighbouring lakes a variety, wholly bright yellow."

Bigsby's narrative continues: "A few miles from the Pewarbic [*Bottle*] Portage, on an island near the south main, there are the remains of a round tower, or defensive building of some sort, twenty-seven feet in diameter. It was erected by the Indians, and commands a wide view of expanses and woody isles. . . . We ascended it [*the Namakan River*] on our return home, entering from a small, quiet bay in Lake Namaycan, full of reeds and water-lilies, its shores lined with long grass and fine young oaks: but when once in the river all is romantic—that is, beautiful and dangerous." He describes the river as "a chain of vehement rapids and still waters; the former pent up in high walls of black basalt, from thirty to sixty yards apart, and crowned with pines; the latter, wide, full of marshy islets, rushes, and lilies."

In ascending this stream the party had to use a tow rope at one of the rapids. Though quite new, it broke and two men in the canoe barely escaped with their lives. Bigsby continues his account: "Just as a bend of the river took our distressed people out of sight, looking up the stream, we saw a long spear erect in the water, and riding rapidly towards us. This I could not at all understand; but in a moment or two there darted down the current, from an upper bend, a canoe in full pursuit, one Indian at the bow, standing aloft on the thwarts, spear in hand; another was guiding. In striking a large fish, it had wrenched the weapon from the hand of the spearsman. . . . There is a fur-collecting post on [*Little*] Lake Vermillion, where the scenery, though sometimes bold, is on the whole softer and more fertile than is common in gneiss districts. . . . We were cheered by noticing five wigwams at an open, pleasant-looking spot."

Bigsby was one of the many physicians who visited this region or traded in it during fur-trade days. Is it merely coincidence that almost invariably the reports of these medical men surpass all other accounts in style, detail, human interest, and exactness? Two other important physicians, Dr. John McLoughlin, the "father of Oregon," and Dr. Charles Borup, also traded in this area.

Fur Trading Companies

BEFORE the days of trusts and cartels, great monopolies made history along the border lakes and elsewhere in the central, western, and northwestern parts of the continent. There the fortunes of men in London, Montreal, and New York were made in the pelts of beaver, muskrat, otter, marten, fisher, wolverine, fox, wolf, bear, and other animals. John Jacob Astor, the founder of the American Fur Company, made no small part of his original fortune in the region of the upper Mississippi and in the border country from Grand Portage and Fond du Lac, now a suburb of Duluth, west and north to the boundary line. His furs were taken down the Great Lakes to New York. There they were shipped to the London, Leipzig, and Canton markets. Transmuted into other goods — for example, into tea in Canton — they became, through resale and reinvestment, the acres of Manhattan on which the Astor fortune rests.

Astor's predecessors and rivals were the Hudson's Bay Company and the North West Company, both of which, like the American Fur Company, operated in the northern part of the Minnesota area. From 1784, when Astor reached America from his native Germany, until the close of the War of 1812, he was unable to get a foothold in the border area because of the long-established control of the other two companies. It was only when the Treaty of Ghent had been signed at the

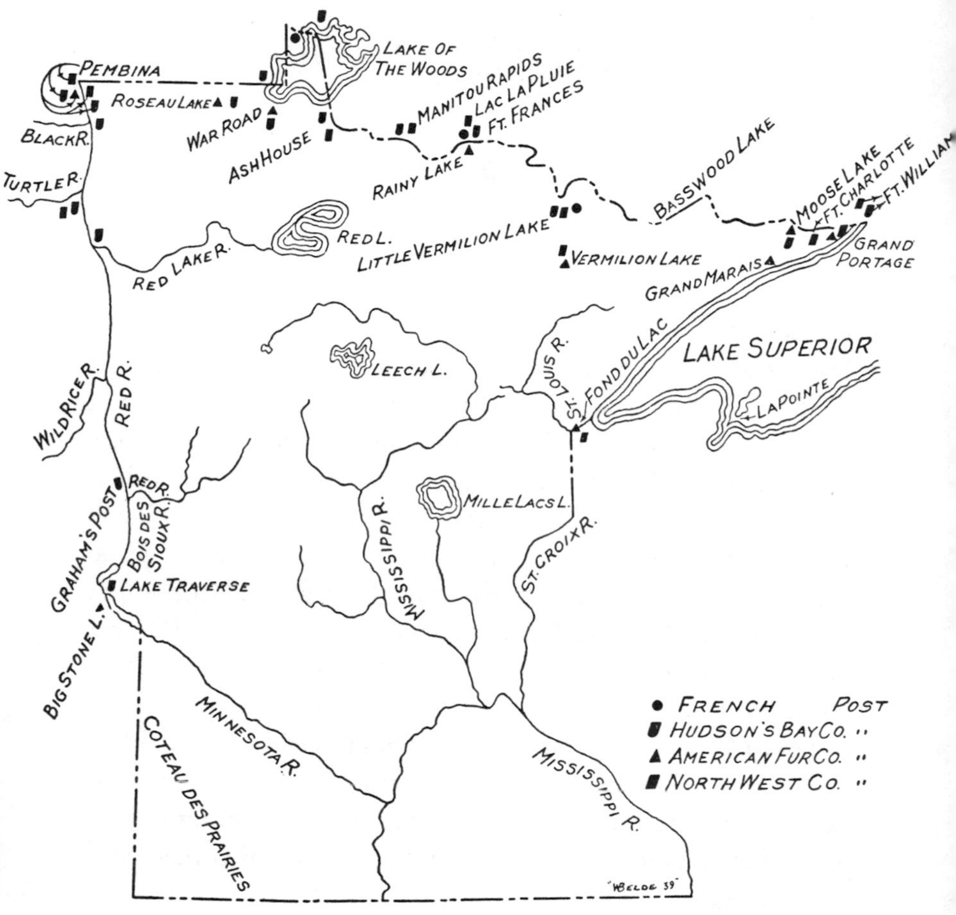

Hudson's Bay Company Trading Sites and Rival Posts in the Minnesota Country

close of the war that Astor's chance came. In 1816 Congress passed an act excluding foreigners from the fur trade, thereby limiting the trade in the border area to Americans. This was a blow to the two British companies, especially to the North West Company. It was already exhausted in a long struggle with the Hudson's Bay Company, part of which had been fought along the historic canoe route that forms the international boundary. Murders and guerrilla warfare played their part in the struggle. The North West Company's posts at Fort William and Rainy Lake were seized by Lord Selkirk of the Hudson's Bay Company. Selkirk's messengers, sent from the Red River settlements across country to Fond du Lac and Montreal, were robbed by rivals. Forty Hudson's Bay men were sent by Lord Selkirk into the Fond du Lac department of the North West Company to trade on the American side of the border. These were but a few of the outrages. The bitterness of the hatred between the men of the two companies is unbelievable today. It even reached the point where an appeal was sent by Astor to the United States government to intervene with troops. A plan was brought forth to establish a United States military post at Fond du Lac to protect the area north to the border from the marauding parties of English traders. The warfare ended in 1821 when the two British companies united under the name of the Hudson's Bay Company.

The North West Company

The ink on the treaty of peace between England and France was hardly dry in 1763, when energetic English and Scotch traders reached the border lakes. Names of many individual traders stand out now instead of being submerged in the general movement, as was true during the French regime. John Askin was clearing a spot for a fort at the Lake Superior end of the Grand Portage by 1768. Jonathan Carver, who was at Grand Portage in the summer of 1767 hoping to continue on his way to the "Ouragan," or Columbia River and the Sea of the West, does not mention Askin's fort; and other evidence points to 1768 as the year of its beginning. So we conclude that the actual clearing began in the latter year. Peter Pond passed over the canoe route in the 1770's and 1780's and went on to the Athabaska country. Soon there were so many traders that murders occurred between rivals, and violence became the order of the day. Out of the cutthroat competition developed a great trading company, one of the three of chief importance in American and Canadian history. This was the North West Company, a loose combination of partnerships, with headquarters in Montreal.

It was the North West Company, from the time of its origin in the late 1770's till 1803, that made the border-lakes canoe route famous the world over. It was also the principal employer of voyageurs. A great inland depot was built at Grand Portage. An important depot fort was constructed also at the other end of the portage and named Fort Charlotte. A fort of special importance, since it was the intermediate terminus of the Athabaska trade, was established at the outlet of Rainy Lake. Way stations and wintering posts were set up at many lesser points along the way, notably at Moose, Knife, Basswood, and Little Vermilion lakes. Every swamp, inlet, rapid, waterfall, portage, and towing spot on the route was given a name by the canoemen. Many of these names remain, though usually in translated or corrupted form.

The Hudson's Bay Company

It was in 1793 that the Hudson's Bay Company entered the Rainy Lake area, or, as it was then called universally, the Lac

A Year-old Black Bear near Ely

A Beaver Dam Northwest of Ely

A Beaver at Work

A Beaver House, Bank Type

Beaver Work, Ottertrack Lake

La Pluie district. The North West Company was already well established, as we have seen. Though Radisson and Des Groseilliers had started the Hudson's Bay Company in 1670, that corporation did not feel Canadian competition sufficiently to take action in the Rainy Lake region till the end of the next century. Posts were then established at the outlet of Rainy Lake and at several points on Rainy River. These lasted only a few years. By 1798 they were gone. Presumably the competition of the Nor' Westers was too strong for "the English," as the older corporation's men were known. In 1818 new posts were erected, after Lord Selkirk, the Scotch founder of a colony on the site of modern Winnipeg and a member of the Hudson's Bay Company, had sent foreign, mostly Swiss, troops to capture the Rainy Lake post from his opponents in 1816.

The Hudson's Bay Company post was at the outlet of Rainy Lake. A wintering house was soon built on Basswood Lake, apparently in 1822. Simon McGillivray, Jr., was the trader for the season of 1822–23. He had as his rival an American probably named Grout, whom McGillivray routed, having seized the Yankee's trading goods. From 1823 to 1825 C. W. Bouck was in charge of the Hudson's Bay Company post on Basswood Lake. Of him it was written at the time that he "knows every Indian of the place their character and disposition – is a good trader and respected by the Indians but has no education." Bouck was in the region as early as 1815. While he served at Basswood he received sixty pounds a year. He had a wife and at least two children. The trader for the company in 1830 was François Mainville; and in 1837–38 and for many years thereafter James Isbister was in charge. Mainville's son was working for a company post on Little Vermilion Lake in 1849, when the geologist Joseph G. Norwood passed; and the same traveler noted a company post on Moose Lake. In general, the company maintained posts on the Canadian side of the border as long as such establishments were profitable. The Hudson's Bay Company and North West Company posts ceased to exist on the American side shortly after the War of 1812, though Indians south of the international line long continued to trade at forts north of the boundary. In 1821 the Hudson's Bay Company engulfed the North West Company and thereafter only the older company had official existence. In 1830 the post at the end of Rainy Lake was named Fort Frances in honor of the bride of Governor George Simpson, who was present with him at the ceremony. The governor, later Sir George Simpson, passed frequently along the canoe route from Fort William to Lac La Croix and on to Rainy Lake and the West.

Douglas MacKay in his book, *The Honourable Company*, lists twelve routes that Simpson followed at various times, including the one from Montreal to Lake Winnipeg by canoe in 1820 and in all but six of the years between 1826 and 1859.

Simpson was one of those extraordinary persons about whom apocryphal stories go on accumulating. Even today one hears remarkable yarns of how fast he traveled by canoe and pack horse across the continent, accompanied by his Scotch piper, using only the finest canoes and the best voyageurs, and making his men perform incredible feats of endurance. The truth is strange enough – whole files of his letters and diaries still in Hudson's Bay Company records in England prove his all-compelling powers of "drive" and personal example – but he has become a legendary figure in the popular mind of Canada. Not least gargantuan of these legends about the "little emperor" is that telling of the number of his dusky offspring along the canoe routes of his far-flung "empire."

Fur Trading Companies

The American Fur Company

Although John Jacob Astor's firm, the American Fur Company with headquarters in New York City, was organized in 1808, it was not until 1823 that it began to establish posts along the border lakes. The first fort was built on Rainy River, opposite the Hudson's Bay Company post at the outlet of Rainy Lake. Soon there were posts farther to the west and a number to the east, notably on Moose, Basswood, Vermilion, and Little Vermilion lakes, and at Grand Portage and Grand Marais.

The post on Basswood Lake was under the supervision of William Aitken, who maintained traders throughout the North Country. Aitken is a well known character in Minnesota history. A county and a town are named for him. Almost as well known was Aitken's lieutenant, William Morrison, for whom another Minnesota county is named. Aitken's trader was at Basswood Lake for several years and probably until 1833, when the Hudson's Bay Company came to an arrangement with the New York firm whereby the sum of three hundred pounds sterling was given to the American Fur Company annually on the promise that the latter company would not carry on the fur trade along the border. This arrangement was maintained till 1847. Thereafter the Hudson's Bay Company had to do all the policing, for the American Fur Company went out of existence about that time. The Hudson's Bay Company proved unequal to the task, Minnesota traders became numerous, and so for several years after 1847 the border was a scene of bitter trade wars.

During the period of the American post at Basswood a colorful person was in charge – Stephen Bonga. His paternal ancestors seem to have been Negro slaves of a British army officer at Mackinac just before the Revolution. Shortly there were many little half-breeds with kinky hair, which is said to have delighted the Indians enormously. Whenever they saw a Negro – the opportunity came seldom – they would place their hands on their hair and laugh merrily. It was customary before the campfires at night for tired voyageurs to recount their own prowess in canoeing and portaging. The tallest tale was told by a Bonga, it is said, who boasted of having carried eight packs across a portage. As the packs, or *pièces*, were made up to weigh ninety pounds each, the measure of his story-telling ability can be gauged. About 1840 Bonga was proving himself an inestimable boon to Methodist missionaries making their first survey of the Chippewa field in the Minnesota country. A circuit rider of note, Alfred Brunson, wrote enthusiastically about Bonga's character and ability at that time. A painting or sketch of this "first white child born at the head of Lake Superior," as Bonga once termed himself, was made in the 1850's by an artist whose works are much sought after today. The Brooklyn Museum exhibited an unusual number of them in 1939. Eastman Johnson was the artist – one of the earliest and best delineators of North Country Indians and half-breeds.

The American traders who reached the border in 1823 were of great interest to the Hudson's Bay Company rivals across the Rainy River. It is diverting to a Minnesotan to read the diaries of the British traders who were in charge of the Canadian post that winter and later. They affect a great disdain for these paltry Americans, though underneath runs a note of fear for the future, especially with respect to the customs collector – a bogey man whom they saw in every new American trader. In 1830 a new face was that of Dr. Charles W. W. Borup. He was the special target for the jibes of one diarist, though his medical education in Copenhagen and wide experience probably exceeded anything that any of the British traders on the border had to offer. The fact that he treated the Indian women like other human beings was far too much for the risibles of the diarist, whose sarcasm and wit were Olympian. History has almost completely forgotten the British diarist, but Dr. Borup is well remembered in the annals of medicine and banking.

Voyageurs

THE VOYAGEURS of the North West Company imparted to the life of the fur-trading regime a sparkle that can be caught even at this distant day. Every year in the early summer brigades of canoes laden with furs and some pemmican passed eastward over the border-lakes canoe route from wintering posts in the South and West, en route to the annual meeting of the North West Company at Grand Portage.[1] In July they returned over the same way to their wintering posts for another season. Thus the border lakes saw twice every season large numbers of staid company partners (*bourgeois*), young clerks (*commis*) training to become *bourgeois*, and canoemen (*voyageurs*). These men wore feather plumes in their caps, or were entitled to do so, for they had been baptized Nor'Westers on their first portage trip across the height of land between North and South Lakes. The baptism was a ceremony never omitted when pork-eaters, as the inexperienced voyageurs were called, or untrained traders passed that way. It consisted of being sprinkled by a cedar bough dipped in water and of promising never to allow a newcomer to get past the portage without a similar experience. Winterers (*hivernants*), who as the name signified had already spent at least one winter in the region,

[1] It was pemmican, the dried and pounded meat of buffaloes, that enabled canoemen to use the Grand Portage canoe route. Food from Canada could not be transported beyond Grand Portage in trade canoes. So pemmican was made at prairie forts, particularly on the Assiniboine River, and shipped by canoe to Grand Portage.

were, of course, exempt from the ritual. After the ceremony, which closed with a salvo of shots, the new Nor'Wester was expected to treat all hands to shrub or high wine — the real object of the affair.

The same reward was in view in another ceremony — the making of a lob pine, or Maypole, as it was frequently called. A pine, usually of great size and prominence, preferably on a height or point of land silhouetted against the sky-line at night, was selected by the voyageurs passing along the canoe route. A man was deputed to climb it, ax in hand, and lop (lob!) off the central branches. Thus the tree was left naked and conspicuous in the middle, a landmark for all future travelers. It was formally named for some individual of the party, usually a *bourgeois* or guest of the group. The person thus honored was expected to respond by giving his canoe mates a liquid treat. Lob pines are said to be still standing on the Kaministikwia route between Fort William and Lac La Croix, on Knife Lake, Cecil Lake, and at other points, lone survivors of a picturesque era now gone forever. One of the important lob pines in trading days was on "Maypole Island" in Rainy Lake.

Down the years echo the canoe songs made famous by North West Company voyageurs. The voyageurs were practically all French Canadians, who inherited the folk songs of the *trouvères* of the Loire Valley, *chansons* which came to Canada with the first settlers in the period between 1608 and 1680. The British and Scotch heads of the company could hardly have carried on the fur trade without these experienced woodsmen, trained in the fur trade for several generations in Canada. French was the language of the trade till toward the close of the nineteenth century, because it was the mother tongue of these voyageurs.

The voyageur sang when he was happy, when he was in danger, when he got up in the morning, as he sat by his campfire at night, when passing through "white water," when at his fort, and especially while he was paddling. He was an effervescent being who took life easily, worked hard, took orders well, assumed little responsibility, got on admirably with the Indians, especially the native women, and gave a fine loyalty to his *bourgeois*. He was an excellent canoeman – better, in fact, than the Indian. His ability to live in the wilderness, make canoes, erect forts, manage huskies, and procure furs made him the mainstay of the trade. And he was chosen in part because of his ability to sing.

The repertoire of the voyageurs included some of the finest folk songs in any language. Most of them are very old. They lose immeasurably by translation, but here are the words and music of a few verses from two of the better known. They must have resounded often against the pines of the border waters as a canoeful of swift-paddling voyageurs sped across the lakes in full song.

EN ROULANT MA BOULE

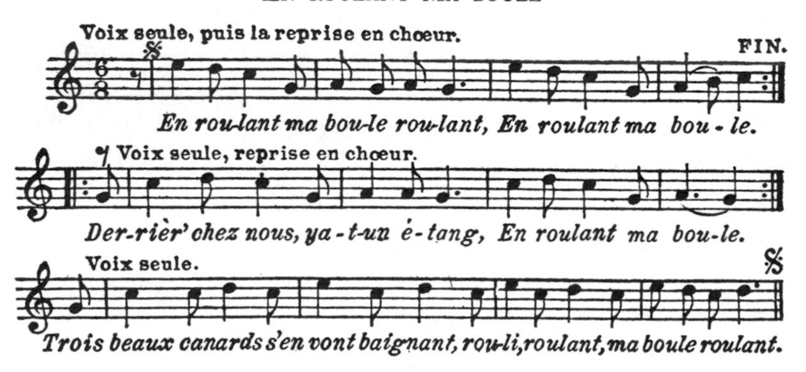

"Encampment on River Winnipeg," a Painting by Paul Kane

A Dog Train on the Gunflint Trail

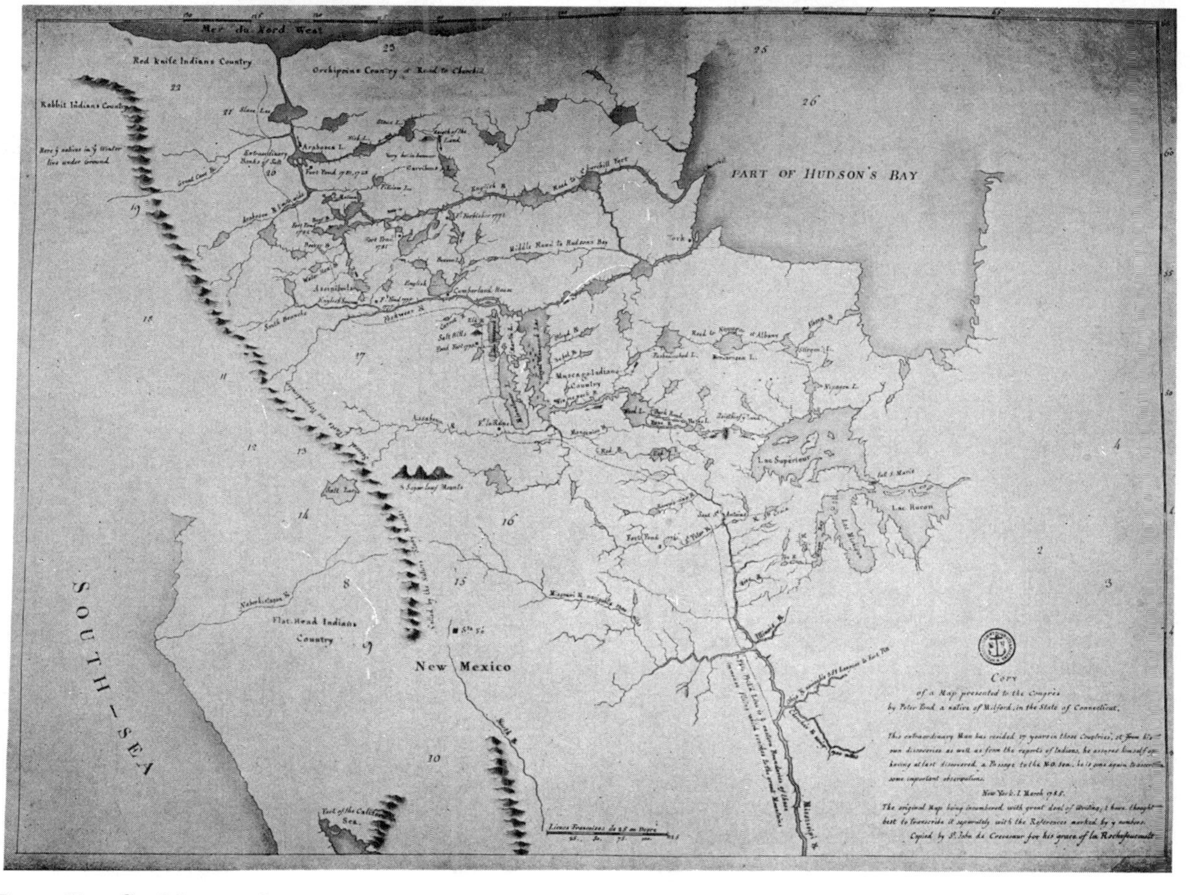

Peter Pond's Map, 1785

Ruffed Grouse

Fawn

En roulant ma boule roulant,
En roulant ma boule.
En roulant ma boule roulant,
En roulant ma boule.

Derrièr' chez nous, ya-t-un étang,
En roulant ma boule.
Derrièr' chez nous, y'-t-un étang,
En roulant ma boule.
Trois beaux canards s'en vont baignant,
Rouli, roulant, ma boule roulant,
En roulant ma boule roulant,
En roulant ma boule.

[Translation] [2]

A-Rolling My Ball

On, roll on, my ball I roll on,
On, roll on my ball, on!
On, roll on, my ball I roll on,
On, roll on my ball, on!

'Way back at home there is a pond,
On, roll on my ball, on!
'Way back at home there is a pond,
On, roll on my ball, on!
Three bonnie ducks go swimming 'round,
Roll on, my ball, my ball I roll on.
On, roll on, my ball I roll on,
On, roll on, my ball, on!

[2] This and the translation of the following song are from J. Murray Gibbon, *Canadian Folk Songs: Old and New*, by permission of the publishers, J. M. Dent and Sons (London, Toronto, and Vancouver), and E. P. Dutton and Company (New York).

A LA CLAIRE FONTAINE

A la claire fontaine
M'en allant promener,
J'ai trouvé l'eau si belle
Que je m'y suis baigné.
Lui ya longtemps que je t'aime,
Jamais je ne t'oublierai.

J'ai trouvé l'eau si belle
Que je m'y suis baigné;
Sous les feuilles d'un chêne
Je me suis fait sécher.
Lui ya longtemps que je t'aime,
Jamais je ne t'oublierai.

[Translation]

AT THE CLEAR RUNNING FOUNTAIN

At the clear running fountain
Sauntering by one day,
I found it so compelling
I bathed without delay.
Your love long since overcame me,
Ever in my heart you'll stay.

I found it so compelling
I bathed without delay;

Under an oak tree's umbrage
I dried the damp away.
Your love long since overcame me,
Ever in my heart you'll stay.

The canoes of the border lakes were smaller than the Montreal canoes, or *canots de maître*, which plied between Montreal and Grand Portage. The smaller craft was called a North canoe, was about twenty-five feet long, and was paddled by from six to ten men including the *bouts*, or the men in either end of the canoe. Of these the bowman (*avant*) stood behind the high gaudily painted prow wielding a long, thin blade. In similar manner the steersman (*gouvernail*) stood in the stern, the most expert of all the canoe's crew. The nimble turn of his wrist at a crucial moment might mean the difference between safety and a watery grave in seething rapids or eddies.

Between the *avant* and the *gouvernail* sat the *milieux*, the run-of-the-mill voyageurs. They simply paddled and sang. They sat in pairs, usually on the ninety-pound bales of trade goods called *pièces*, and swung paddles that were much shorter than those of the *bouts*. The paddle blades were usually painted red, and it must have been a stirring sight to see six to ten men pushing forward a great, loaded canoe with their red paddles flashing in the sunlight, a stroke every second.

Several men were needed to portage a large Montreal canoe, which had to be carried bottom up. The Montreal canoes were exchanged at Grand Portage for the smaller North canoes, which could be carried right side up by only two men. The portages were hard, weary stretches for the voyageurs, though their picturesque names have poetic appeal to us who pore over maps of the North Country more than a hundred years later. From Montreal to Lake Superior, via the Ottawa River, Lake Nipissing, and French River, there were thirty-six portages; from Grand Portage to Rainy Lake there were thirty-six more; and from Rainy Lake to Lake Winnipeg there were twenty-six. In order, from Grand Portage to Basswood Lake, the chief portages were: the Partridge, Big Rock, Caribou, Fowl, Moose, Big Cherry, Vaseux, Little Cherry, Little New (now Watap), Big New (Long), Marten, Perch, Height of Land, Staircase, Wooden Horse, Prairie (Swamp), the three Knife portages, Carp and Big Basswood (Prairie).

Beyond Basswood Lake the portages as far as Rainy Lake were: Little Basswood and Big Pine (which together are now Horse), Wood Point (Wheelbarrow), Little Rock (Lower Falls), Curtain, Bottle, three in Lac La Croix, two New, and Kettle Falls. These portage names are even more picturesque and euphonious in their French form. The voyageur had a big dash of poetry in his make-up and it was nowhere more apparent than in the names he gave topographical features.

Over the many portages the canoes and their lading had to be carried. Sweating, panting, dark with mud, and covered with mosquito and fly bites, the voyageurs dogtrotted, punctuating the carriage with many a *sacré*. Two or three bales, or 180 to 270 pounds of goods, were held on the bent back by a portage strap, which passed around the voyageur's forehead and reached to the small of his back. The entire crossing was seldom made in one carriage, unless the portage was a very short one. It was usually broken up into *poses*, or places of deposit, as the term can be awkwardly translated. In other words, stations were recognized, to which all the goods and the canoe were brought and put down (*posé*) before the next stretch was begun. So a portage was seldom spoken of by voyageurs as being so many feet or leagues in length; instead, it was mentioned as being a portage of say, three or five *poses*.

The voyageur also had his own terminology for other

phases of his life. Basswood Lake, for example, would not be described by him as twenty eight miles in length but as a lake of four *pipes*, or rest periods. The arduous work of paddling a loaded canoe was relieved about every hour by respites of perhaps ten minutes. During the recess the men brought out clay pipes, tobacco, steel, and flint, and lighted up. Then, after their smoke, it was back to their paddles and their song, when pipes and their accessories had been returned to beaded pouches hanging from fringed sashes (*ceintures flèchées*) about the paddlers' waists.

Once in the interior, the trader and his voyageurs made their way as expeditiously as possible to their fort. All trading posts were called "forts," if they were enclosed by pickets. In fact, in voyageur parlance the fort was the stockade. Usually several wintering houses depended on a fort. Thus the Hudson's Bay Company post at the outlet of Rainy Lake maintained at least the following dependent stations, or wintering houses: Basswood Lake, Little Vermilion Lake, Manitou Rapids, Ash House near the mouth of Rainy River, several establishments on Lake of the Woods, Warroad, and a few posts north of Rainy River. The North West Company post at Rainy Lake had a similar set of dependent posts.

A house was put up rapidly for a wintering post. Thus, on October 7, 1794, the Ash House foundations were laid, twenty-five feet by twenty within the walls, as the diaries of the Rainy Lake post in London reveal. On the ninth "the House [was] 5 logs high." On the tenth Indians assisted the whites to carry stones for the chimneys. By the eleventh the house was seven logs high. On the fourteenth the men "put the girders on the house." The next day "the people [were] putting the Rige on the house." The following day they were "putting on the Roof," which was thatched with hay. On the seventeenth the gable ends were completed. The stone work of the chimneys was done on the nineteenth and the clay work for one of them on the twentieth. By the twenty-second the chimneys were finished. The bedroom floors, the "upper floor," and the hearth in the bedroom were finished on the twenty-ninth. The following day was spent by the "people laying floor of the Big room." So the house required about a month to complete, with hearths, good clay and stone chimneys, well-laid floors of sawed lumber, window shutters, and so on. Windows were usually of oiled parchment. A trench was dug for the palisades, which were probably of the usual height, approximately fifteen feet above ground and three feet below. Besides the house proper, there was undoubtedly a "shop" at Ash House and very likely the customary house for the voyageurs. The houses in the area were all built substantially alike, whether they belonged to the North West Company, the Hudson's Bay Company, or the American Fur Company.

The exact manner of putting the logs in place and keeping them there without nails is of special interest because it was quite unlike the usual American method of the present time. The procedure is graphically described in the following letter, written by a missionary, the Reverend Sherman Hall, from La Pointe on Lake Superior on September 30, 1832:

> You inquire respecting the manner of building in this country. You are aware I suppose that the Indians build no kind of timbered houses. . . . The timbered houses are therefore built by those who come to this country for trade. You are also aware that we have no mills of any kind for sawing timber or grinding grain. All timber for building must be prepared by hand. A few buildings are reared nearly in the old Yankee manner of building log houses, that is, of round timbers locked together at the ends. The most common method however, is to build with hewed timber. There is a great abundance of good building timber almost

everywhere in this country. When a building is to be put up, the timber for the sills, beams & posts is cut and squared into suitable sticks, usually with a common axe, for a hewer's broad axe is seldom seen here, and no body knows how to use it. The sills & beams are generally locked or halfed together at the corners of the building, for few can frame them together with tenant and mortice. A mortice is made in the sill for a post wherever it is needed & an other in the beam. A groove is made in each post from top to bottom about 2 inches in width, and three or four inches deep. Timbers are then hewed six or seven inches thick and the ends cut till they are fitted to the groove in the post, and of sufficient length to reach from one post to another. They are then introduced one after another till the walls of the building are completed. These timbers answer every purpose answered by studs, braces, and boarding in the English mode of building. Wherever a window or a door is required, posts are erected, into which the ends of the timbers are introduced, instead of the main posts, and thus the required hole is made in the wall. A post is placed at the centre of each end of the building which is continued above the beam as high as the top of the roof is intended to be. A stick of timber is then laid on the top of these posts reaching from one end of the building to the other, and forms the ridge pole. The roof is then formed by laying one end of timbers on this ridge pole and the other on the plate till the whole is covered. These timbers answer the purpose of boards on the roofs of English buildings. For shingling cedar barks are used. These barks are taken from the white cedar which is plenty, in this part of the country, in the early part of summer. A single piece from 4 to 5 feet in length is pealed from each tree which is left standing. It is smooth bark, not thick, rather stringy, and not brittle when dry. These barks are put upon the timbers of the roof in the manner of shingles, and are secured by narrow strips of board which are laid across them and spiked to the timbers. A roof of this kind will last several years. The cracks between the timbers in the walls are plastered with a hard clay which abounds in this country and are then covered with cedar bark in the manner of the roof, if the building is intended for a house.

Hall then goes on to describe the making of boards for the interior of the house – floors, partitions, and so on. His account of how a pit saw operated is unusually explicit. There was a pit saw at the Rainy Lake post very early in the nineteenth century. It was used for making the boards for the large North West Company post there.

In Hall's reminiscences, written many years later and published in a Sauk Rapids newspaper in the sixties, he goes on with his account of how these voyageur log houses were constructed: "The chimney was made of clay, first worked up into morter, then made into rolls twenty inches long and four in diameter, with straw or hay worked into them to hold them together. These are put on a framework of upright poles and cross sticks, and moulded and rubbed and worked by hand, piece after piece, and layer after layer, till at length they form a chimney. – And no other chimney did I ever see used in that country till I had been there fifteen years."[4]

[4] Life in border forts may be found described in the diary, or journal, kept at every post. Many of these volumes have survived. Several that relate to the northern Minnesota country – the diaries of five fur traders and the reminiscences of Peter Pond – have been edited by Charles M. Gates and published as *Five Fur Traders of the Northwest* (Minneapolis, 1933). One of the five traders was John Macdonell, who passed over the border lakes in 1793. His vivid and illuminating descriptions are our best account of voyageur travel customs. The most valuable of the diaries from the point of view of this sketch of the region between Rainy Lake and Grand Portage is that of Hugh Faries, kept at the North West Company's post at Rainy Lake in the season of 1804–05. Day by day this clerk wrote down the minutiae of life at his fort and at the numerous wintering posts dependent upon it, which dotted the wilderness toward Lake Superior in one direction and toward Lake of the Woods in the other. It is a very human document, full of Indians who are real beings, not animals, noble savages, or some other figment of a writer's imagination; full of voyageurs of all types, ages, conditions, and outlook on life; full of merrymakings, tragedies, and humdrum existence; and replete with keen interest in forest life, fishing, hunting, and the appearance of the countryside. It refers to gardens, domestic animals, the canoe yard, the cooper making staves for rice and fish barrels, the saw pit, and other appurtenances of the fort. From it one can form a clear picture of life at a border post.

Tall Timber

Lake Trout

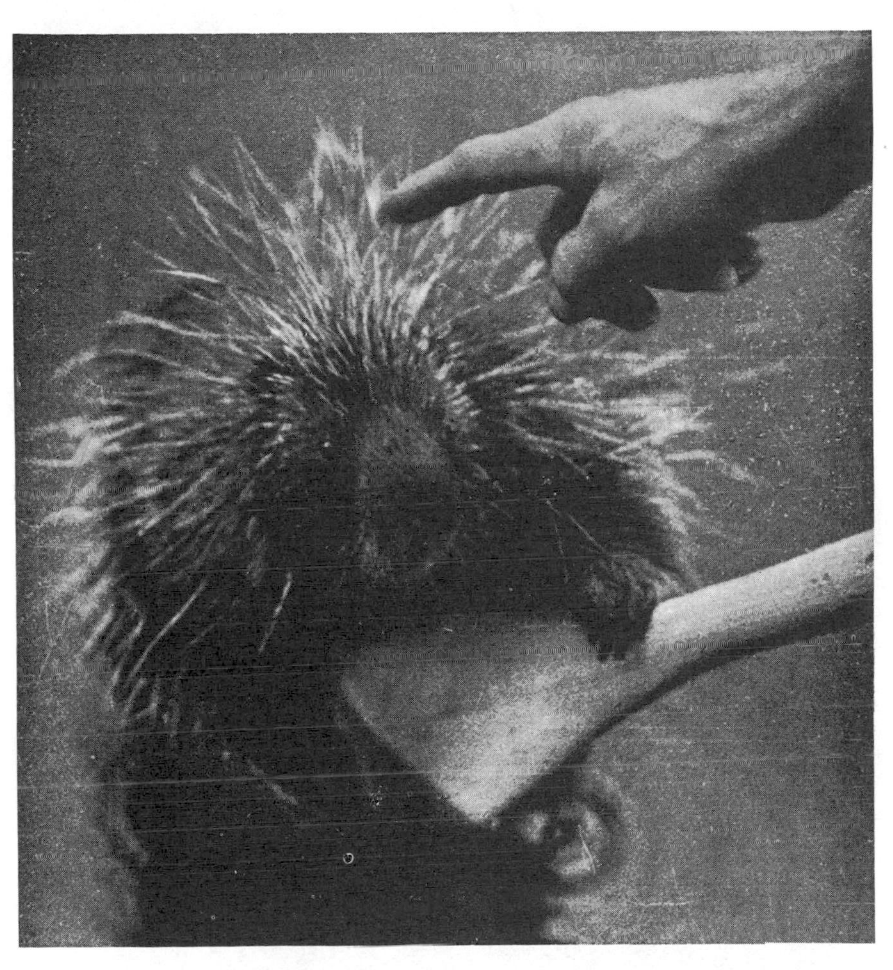

A Porcupine on a Paddle

Stemless Lady's-Slipper

Border Indians

FEW AREAS of the United States can boast as varied an Indian history as northern Minnesota. Who the first natives were is uncertain, but most anthropologists today incline to the view that they were of Siouan stock, the mound builders. When they came and when they left is unknown. When the first white men entered the region about 1660, the forest Sioux, as distinguished from the plains Sioux, were in possession. But already they were being forced back by men of another great linguistic stock, the Algonquian. These were the Cree, Monsoni, and Chippewa, the last known also as the Ojibway. By 1750 the Sioux had been forced out of most of the forested area, the Cree and the Monsoni had moved a little farther north and northwest, and the Chippewa were masters of nearly all the forest region. Unlike the Sioux, who were obliged to leave Minnesota after their uprising against the white settlers in 1862, the Chippewa have remained in northeastern and northern Minnesota. The chief groups now within the region south and east of Rainy Lake are the Bois Fort band, whose reservation is at Nett Lake, and the Grand Portage band.

The Chippewa seldom killed white men. In this respect they differed notably from such tribes as the Iroquois and the Sioux. They were and are a pleasant, fun-loving people, speaking a language notable for its intricacies, softness, and richness of vocabulary. It was the "polite" language of the continent, like French among modern Europeans.

The Chippewa's typical house was a wigwam, or dome-shaped structure of saplings covered with rush and bark mats. Two other types of house were fairly common, however: the conical tepee, borrowed from the Sioux; and a sort of elongated tepee structure, or long house.

The food of the Chippewa in the northeastern part of Minnesota consisted of three main items: game, fish, and, as vegetable material, wild rice, berries, and maple sugar.

The accounts and diaries of early traders make it apparent that the Indians knew exactly when the fishing in any lake was best. George Monk, a trader writing of northern Minnesota about the year 1807, gives the periods when it was desirable to go to this or that lake for certain fish. In parts of the Rainy Lake basin the sturgeon fisheries were famous. The Indians speared these fish or actually caught them with their hands. Seines also were used on occasion, especially after traders entered the region. Whitefish were numerous and were great favorites. Pike, both walleyed and northern, were secured in summer as well as through the ice in winter. Other fish, especially bass and trout, also were taken. In Rainy Lake and a few other lakes to the south and west of it a tullibee found only in this region was caught. It is a species of whitefish and is often mentioned by early traders.

Fish remain to this day one of the chief attractions of the region. Thousands of fishing licenses are issued every year. The Liars' Club draws heavily for membership on fishermen from the north woods. Probably the three most-sought-after fish are walleyed pike, bass, and lake trout. Great northern pike and muskellunges are large and full of fight. There are many other varieties. No one who has bobbed about in a canoe in the swirl of fast water below falls hoping to take walleyed pike—and then has landed them and cooked them over a campfire under a great pine—will fail to understand why the Chippewa love their homeland, especially their lakes and streams.

The region is still a home, though a greatly diminished and impoverished one, for many of the animals that the Indians hunted before the white man arrived and for two centuries thereafter. The caribou had practically disappeared a few years ago, but efforts are now being made to bring them back. The tourist is a poor observer who today fails to note the great, cowlike prints of moose on the portage trails, or in a stay of any length to encounter deer in abundance, varying hare, muskrat, skunk, black bear, beaver, and porcupine. The mink, fox, wolf, and weasel are still common, and occasionally one may see an otter, fisher, or lynx. The wolverine, the wily scourge of the trapper's lines, fortunately has gone.

The beaver, which, like the other animals, supplied the Indians with both food and clothing, became nearly extinct at the beginning of the nineteenth century as the result of the great forest fires of 1803 and 1804, the depredations of wolverines, and certain obscure diseases which puzzled Indians and traders then as they have mystified biologists ever since. An attempt at restocking was made about 1825 by the Rainy Lake trading post under Dr. John McLoughlin, but the Sturgeon Lake Indians pilfered the "resting" beaver lodges and spoiled a noble effort. Of the forest fires J. D. Cameron, the Hudson's Bay Company trader at Rainy Lake in 1826, wrote that in 1803 and 1804 "the whole Country almost from one extremity to the other was in a Continual blaze and stopt only by the snows of autumn." Today beaver are becoming plentiful again under the system of trapping control and permit tags. Many of their dams and houses may be encountered on almost any canoe trip. The patient visitor can even see beavers at work, if he will sit motionless long enough in an area where they are cutting. A loud slap of the water with a broad tail will be a defiant beaver's response to the tiniest movement or human sound, however, as the wary animal disappears beneath the surface.

The best early accounts of the fauna of the region are supplied by Dr. McLoughlin in his sketch of the Little Vermilion Lake country, where he was operating as a trader about 1807, and in his report for the whole Rainy Lake district in 1823 to the Hudson's Bay Company. The first of these will bear quoting: "The Fish caught in these lakes and Rivers, is Sturgeon, Pike, Pickerel, White Fish, trout and Sucker. . . . The Animals that haunt these forests are the moose or Elk, Reindeer or carebou, wolf, wolverine, Fisher, lynx, marten, Bear, Fox, and Hare. Those of the Amphibious kind are the Beaver, Muskrat, and Mink. . . . As to their [*Indians'*] food, it consists of flesh and fish with the addition in some places of wild Rice, which is the Only Kind of pulse they have." McLoughlin's report of 1823 opens with a very long, fine description of the region, and a list of the local Indians. He indicates whether each native hunted north or south of the boundary line, which of them were good hunters, whether they were honest, and so forth. He found 107 men, 118 women, and 230 children. His report adds that the principal fur-bearing animals on which he and his subordinates made their returns were "the martens and muskratts." Reindeer and moose were present, he stated, but in such small numbers that the natives could not kill enough "to supply themselves with leather for their Mogosins and snow Shoes." Thereupon he lists the other animals and adds, "Beaver . . . has been diminishing for these several years past, especially on the South Side of Rainy Lake – Rainy River and Lake of the Woods."

The wild rice attracted huge flocks of geese and mallards, bluebills, redheads, teal, and other ducks in the fall. Birds still nest in great numbers, and in spring and fall the lakes, streams, and forests are alive with great flocks of migrants whose nesting grounds are farther north.

The wild rice, so beloved of waterfowl, is a beautiful annual, a sort of wild oats known to scientists as *Zizania aquatica*. It grows in the soft ooze of glacial lakes and ponds and in the alluvial beds of slow-moving streams. It provided food for many of the Indian tribes east of the Rocky Mountains, particularly those in Wisconsin and northern Minnesota. Blossoms appear in June, the kernels ripen in August, and in September the rice is harvested and prepared for storage by interesting native methods. Today the methods are practically those of untold earlier generations. Let a man who early watched the Indians at harvest time, Dr. McLoughlin, writing from Little Vermilion Lake about 1807, describe the process of gathering the rice:

"Wild Rice call'd by the Natives Ma-no-mien grows in Shallow lakes with a Muddy mixt with a Sandy bottom and in the water along the banks of Rivers It is ripe in the Month of September They go through it with their small canoes and with a Stick they bend the Stem over the Canoe, and with an other beat the husk so that the grain falls in the canoe, then place it over a small fire on hay or Small willows for to dry by degrees – after which they place it in holes dug in the Ground and lin'd with dress'd Skins and pound it with a Mortar or trample it with their feet till the Chaf leaves the Grain then van [*winnow*] it and it is fit for use One quart of the Grain boil'd in two Gallons of any kind of Broth or in the same quantity of water with an ounce of Grease till it come to a consistence of porridge or rather thinner is in General as much as any man will Eat in a day. Their [*sic*] is an other Way of prepareing oats. It is collected in the same way as the other but before it is Ripe, and then dried in a Kettle stiring it about continually untill it leaves the chaff. Then van'd as the other this is call'd Roastd Oats and it requires at least three pints of this to answer to two of the other Besides this they Eat a kind of Excrescence [*moss*] that grows on Rocks call'd by the natives trippe de Roche and a species of wood call'd by the same people *Bois tors* [*bittersweet*] and the sap of the Birch."

It is not generally known that birch sap can be used to make sugar. The Chippewa use it for that purpose even today. The birch was used also for another purpose. Throughout the border country grew canoe birches, the bark from which was necessary for making canoes. Rainy Lake birches even entered diplomatic dispatches when the British fur traders in the 1790's roundly told the Canadian government that the western boundary between Canada and the United States, as outlined by the treaty of peace of 1783, was a great mistake, and that the line must be rerun so that Rainy Lake birches would still be British and available for trade canoes.

McLoughlin failed to mention one interesting step sometimes taken in the harvesting of wild rice. Before the heads of the grain were ripe, the natives pushed their canoes into the rice fields and tied bunches of heads together all over the fields. The purpose of this procedure was to keep winds from shaking out the kernels as they ripened and became loose and to prevent the great flocks of geese and ducks from securing the better part of the harvest. By 1939, wild rice had become very popular as an article of American diet – so much so that commercial companies were despoiling the fields and leaving little for seed and the birds. Hence the Minnesota legislature passed an act in 1939, which was amended in 1941, to permit the conservation department of the state to reverse the Indians' procedure by helping to reseed and assisting the birds to secure their share of the rice crop by limiting the activities of rice traders.

Blueberries grew where fires had swept, particularly on denuded hill slopes. The natives probably set some fires to insure good blueberry crops. The berries not used immediately by the Indians were dried in the sun or in the smoke of fires and, like wild rice, were cached for later use. Cranberries were sunk in freezing water and thus preserved, anticipating our frozen foods of today. The Indian name for Basswood Lake is "Passeau-Minac-Sagaigan," if we accept Alexander Mackenzie's spelling. It means "Dried Berry Lake." Today many Indians still visit its shores and neighboring hills in July and August to pick blueberries.

The sap of the maple has already been mentioned. Though few hard maples grew in the northern part of the border country, it is probably correct to mention maple sugar as another product of the area in general which made it so desirable to the Indians. As soon as the long-looked-for crow, the first bird of spring, was seen, usually late in March, the Indian women began to make plans for the happiest portion of their year, the sugar season. Off to the sugar bush they moved, bag and baggage, while the men went muskrat hunting. All through April the sap of the maple tree was running, and hard, exhausting work was the lot of the women, as they tapped the trees, carried birch-bark vessels (*makuks*) of sap to the fires, and chopped wood for the kettles that must be kept boiling day and night. Yet they loved their sugar making and, as one of their missionaries remarked, "no power and no money could keep them from it."

Other trees and plants of great importance to the Indians were the white cedar, the spruce, one of the reeds, and the dogwood. The wood of the white cedar was used for the framework of their canoes, which were smaller and lighter than the Montreal or even the North canoes of the traders. It was used also for canoe paddles. The roots of the spruce were dug by Indian women, split, and used for thread for sewing the seams of bark utensils and canoes. This thread was called *wattape*, or *watab*, by the Chippewa. The resin of the spruce was used for gumming the seams of bark canoes. The inner bark of the dogwood served as tobacco and was the genuine *kinnikinnick*. The reed was the basis of the mats woven by Indian women for the lower walls and floors of their lodges.

As to the number of Indians in the region, we have already noted Dr. McLoughlin's estimate. Mackenzie, one hundred and fifty years ago, noted how few were the Indians about Basswood Lake. He explains the phenomenon thus: "Before the small-pox ravaged this country [*in 1780*], and completed, what the Nodowasis [*Sioux*], in their warfare, had gone far to accomplish, the destruction of its inhabitants, the population was very numerous: this was also a favourite part, where they made their canoes, etc., the lake abounding in fish, the country round it being plentifully supplied with various kinds of game, and the rocky ridges, that form the boundaries of the water, covered with a variety of berries. . . . Since that period, the few people remaining, who were of the Algonquin nation, could hardly find subsistence; game having become so scarce, that they depended principally for food upon fish and wild rice, which grows spontaneously in these parts."

Eastman Johnson's Sketch of Kennewawbemint, a Chippewa Indian, about 1857

Chippewa Canoe Building: Shaping the Canoe

Chippewa Canoe Building: Sewing the Gunwales with Wattape

Indian Graves

Joe Boshey, a Chippewa Indian, about Ninety-five Years Old

Dr. McLoughlin made this further comment about the Indians of his district in 1823: "The Indians of this District have lost a good deal of that Bold independent Spirit which characterized the Sauteux nation of which they are a Tribe. This has been caused by the Competition amongst the Traders who were in the habit of encouraging the Indians to defraud their Creditors. Yet there are many who will not cheat their Traders and spoil, as they term it, their Body."

An Indian Captive

JUST as the United States was adopting a constitution, a blue-eyed lad of some ten years, John Tanner, was stolen by Indians from his father's stockaded cabin in Kentucky, near the mouth of the Miami River. He was fairly well treated by his kidnapers, since it was for adoption by a bereaved Indian mother, the Otter Woman, that he had been abducted. "Shaw-shaw-wabe-nase" (the Falcon) he now became. By that name he was to be known for thirty years among the Indians. After a few years, he was adopted a second time and taken by his new foster mother, Net-no-kwa, to her husband, Taw-ga-we-ninne (the Hunter), a Chippewa of the Red River country.

After thirty years among the Indians of Minnesota's border waters, Tanner returned to civilization at Sault Ste. Marie, where a well-known army doctor, Edwin James, took down the story of the captive from his own lips. It is probably the most authentic picture of Indian life through Indian eyes that has come to us. For Tanner became an Indian in all respects save blood. The Indian's language, craft, and point of view became his. He married an Indian woman and had Indian children, one of whom, James Tanner, became a well-known missionary to his own people in Minnesota and the Dakotas.

Fortunate it is for us that his story was printed. Reading it we are back on the border lakes, under great pines, skimming the waters in canoes of our own construction. Our companions are our Indian father, mother, brothers and sisters, relatives, and friends. We stalk the moose, one of the wariest beasts of the forest, for which we have the greatest respect. Again, we go on the war path deep into Minnesota's southern territory. We endure famine and face starvation frequently. We hunt the buffalo, break up beaver houses, make maple sugar, gather wild rice, go on drunken frolics, and get cheated by the numerous English and American traders. And always and ever we are on the move. Again and again we pass rapidly over the surfaces of Rainy, La Croix, and Basswood lakes, frequently in rain. Often we are held wind-bound on their islands and shores.

This pseudo-Indian noted the animals, birds, and fishes of his hunting grounds. Of one early period he tells: "Afterwards, I directed my attention more to the hunting of beaver. I knew of more than twenty gangs of beaver in the country about my camp, and I now went and began to break up the lodges, but I was much surprised to find nearly all of them empty. At last I found that some kind of distemper was prevailing among these animals, which destroyed them in vast numbers. . . . Many of them, which I opened, were red and bloody about the heart. Those in large rivers and running water suffered less; almost all of those that lived in ponds and stagnant water, died. Since that year [*about 1800*] the beaver have never been so plentiful in the country of Red River and Hudson's Bay, as they used formerly to be."

Those who are under the illusion that Indians were always generous and just with one another should read the many instances like the following, which are given throughout Tanner's volume: "In about a month that I remained here [*near Pembina River*] . . . I killed, notwithstanding the poorness of my gun, twenty-four bears, and about ten moose. Having now a great deal of bear's fat, which we could not eat, I visited the *sunjegwun* [*cache*] I had made, where I killed the twenty moose, with seven balls, and put the fat into it. At length, when provisions became very scarce, I returned with my family to this place, expecting to live until spring on the meat I had saved; but I found that Wa-me-gon-a-biew, with his own family, and several others, had been there, broken it open, and taken away every pound of meat." He describes many such caches, one of which he constructed of logs so tightly that not even a mouse could get in.

Encounters with bears and other wild animals become simple but effective dramas. The representative of the Prophet comes among the natives, preaching a new religion that profoundly stirs the simple Indian minds.[1] The arrival in 1812 of white women at Lord Selkirk's colony, where Winnipeg now is, is mentioned: "Among these I saw, for the first time in many years, since I had become a man, a white woman." The contracting of a devastating disease from these settlers, which killed many of the Indians and from which Tanner and his wife suffered long, the kindness of Dr. McLoughlin at the Rainy Lake post of the Hudson's Bay Company, and the passing of exploring parties and boundary commissioners are related.

Finally Tanner returned to civilization and became United States interpreter at Sault Ste. Marie. He died under peculiar circumstances and probably undeserved suspicion attending the murder of James Schoolcraft, the brother of the more famous Henry R. Schoolcraft.

[1] The Prophet, a brother of Tecumseh, was inspiring not only a new religion but another Indian war similar to Pontiac's Conspiracy when the War of 1812 opened. That event merged the Indian war with the general conflict, so that little attention has been given by historians to the Indian revolt.

Physical Features

Geological History

Geologically the North Country bows to none in interest. It is a part of the oldest land mass in the world and is the southwestern end of the Laurentian Highland or Canadian Shield. It has passed through all the earth-building eras of the earth, beginning with the Archeozoic age, when the crust of the earth was thin and it was easy for the molten interior to spill out through rifts in the rocks. When this land mass was formed the earth rotated more rapidly than at present. Consequently days were shorter than twenty-four hours. Here too grew the earliest plants. The ocean submerged this area again, not once but several times. Finally a range of high mountains emerged. Aeons passed and they were eroded down to the metamorphic and igneous rocks at their bases, which now form the surface in this region. When you see Tower Hill and Jasper Peak, you are beholding the slight remains of the old Minnesota Mountains. Next followed lava flows of greenstone and basalt and finally intrusions of various granitic rocks. Again weathering and erosion wore down the rocks, leaving the iron ores, the granites, and the lava flows. Millions of years later several ice sheets passed over this country, where evidences of them are common. One can see the glacial scratches on many of the dome-shaped outcrops.

In geological parlance the oldest rock in the column, lying beneath all the others, is the Archean. Until the so-called Vermilion iron-bearing district of Minnesota was studied by geologists, Archean rock was usually considered to be entirely igneous in character; that is, that it was the result of great heat caused usually by volcanic fire and pressure. Now it is known that it sometimes includes sedimentary rock, as in this district. Underlying all rocks here is the Ely greenstone. In it and above it is found the iron-bearing Soudan formation, which was deposited in the Archean sea. A folding process then enveloped it in the greenstone. Then this disseminated iron was carried by percolating waters, which leached out silica as they went, providing space for ore deposits. The largest known deposits are at Ely and they are typical of the iron ore that lies at the bottom of the sedimentary rocks and immediately on the greenstone.

Within the Ely greenstone and the Soudan formation today one finds granites, which are much younger than either and which have been intruded as dikes into both. They are known as the granites of Vermilion, Trout, Burntside, and Basswood lakes, the granite between Moose Lake and the Kawishiwi River, and the granite of Saganaga Lake. These are acid igneous rocks and are very old, though younger by far than the greenstone. When you see them in your canoe trips on these waters, rising as cliffs or forcing you to portage, remember that you are beholding or treading on some of the oldest substance on earth.

Drainage Basins, Rivers, and Lakes

Here is one of the chief watersheds of the continent. Waters start in this region that end in the Atlantic, the Arctic, and the Gulf of Mexico. Most of them drain to Rainy Lake and proceed on by Rainy River, Lake of the Woods, the Winnipeg River, Lake Winnipeg, and Nelson River to Hudson Bay. Others take waters down to Lake Superior and so to the St. Lawrence and the Atlantic. Near by, just to the south and west, is the Mississippi, some of whose tributaries begin in the vicinity of Hibbing and Chisholm on the Mesabi Range. This North Country, then, is the ridgepole of the continent.

Until the geology of this area had been studied, it was believed that Minnesota's thousands of lakes were practically all formed by glacial action. Hundreds of lakes in the Vermilion district, between Gunflint Lake and the west end of Vermilion Lake, disprove this conception. There all the large lakes and many of the small ones owe their origin to preglacial erosion, which scoured out deep valleys, nearly all of which trend northeast and southwest. Across these valleys, drift from the glaciers that swept down from the Arctic in relatively modern times made dams at intervals, against which water backed up and formed lakes.

The lakes in the eastern portion of the Vermilion district are more numerous than in the western section. Some in both sections are of great size. Vermilion Lake, the largest, is about seventy square miles in area. Basswood Lake has a very intricate shore line several hundred miles in length; its extension from east to west is about fifteen miles, with long, deep bays and some four hundred islands of all sizes. Saganaga Lake is also large. Its geological history is especially interesting and unusual. In all, some two thousand lakes are reported for the district.

The northeast-southwest trend of the lakes in this district was fortunate for fur traders and geologists, for it meant a diagonal canoe route. Traders could make the trip of seventy-five miles or so from Vermilion Lake to Gunflint Lake in a straight line by a route of only twenty portages aggregating in all not more than four miles of carriage. Some of these portages are mere lifts and others are only from ten to fifty yards in length.

The lakes in the western part of the Vermilion district are usually shallow and their waters are often dark in color. Their shores and drainage basins are frequently swampy. Muskegs are common. It is material dissolved from swamp vegetation that produces the dark color of the water. In the eastern part of the district, on the contrary, the lakes are deep and have very small drainage basins and but few swamps. So they are crystal clear. In them are found trout and bass as full of fight as any sportsman can wish.

Forests

West of a line drawn from the western end of Knife Lake to Ensign, Snowbank, Moose, and North Twin lakes, and thence to the Kawishiwi River, the forest growth before lumbering operations commenced was heavy and old and of mixed growth – large areas of white and Norway pines interspersed with birches in great numbers and many poplars, jack pines, spruces, balsam firs, tamaracks, and white cedars. There was very little undergrowth. Fires had taken a heavy toll here even before logging began late in the last century. In fact, certain tracts were known as the "Burned Forties." Some of the fires occurred between 1880 and 1900, but others took place much earlier. There are extensive cranberry marshes in this district.

The eastern section of the district was partially denuded of its forests by successive fires. A clue to one period of conflagration about Gunflint Lake is given in government survey records, which report fires in the 1860's. However, there are accounts of even earlier ones. Dr. McLoughlin wrote of the

A Bull Moose

Birches

Aspen Lace

Reindeer Moss near Ely

Because of forest-fire prevention and control this moss is becoming plentiful again on rocky outcroppings of the Superior National Forest and the Quetico Provincial Park areas, after widespread destruction by fire a generation ago. It has played an important part in the history of the area, for it begins the breaking down of rock into soil and it is the staple article in the caribou's diet. It is thought that the destruction of the moss was a main cause of the disappearance of the caribou from the area. It is of slow growth. After the receding of the caribou herds, moose became numerous; but they, too, diminished in number with the advent of lumbering and the encroachment of civilization in the late nineteenth and early twentieth centuries. Deer began to enter the region about 1890. They are now common, and there is evidence that the caribou is beginning to return.

region between Lake Superior and Lake of the Woods: "The soil is variable in some places only sand, but in general it is fine and mix'd with a small portion, of Clay or a Kind of white Earth over which their [*sic*] is about an Inch of Black Mould, but along the banks of some Rivers and in some low places it is from six to twelve Inches. This mould is form'd from leaves and Rotten wood. In the Summer when dry it burns like wood, and as by the carelessness of the Natives, the fire runs in some part of the country every year it happens that that low Ground by being moist Escapes, while the hills Burn."

Mineral Resources

In 1849 the United States geologist, David Dale Owen, sent his assistant, Joseph G. Norwood, through various parts of Minnesota – along a portion of the north shore of Lake Superior, up the old canoe route from Grand Portage to Saganaga Lake, up the St. Louis River and through Vermilion Lake to Rainy Lake, and into other areas. At the entrance of Namakan Lake he noted and reported a point called by the Indians "Wabisegon." There he saw an exposure of mica slate with feldspar veins that resembled a snake and in consequence was regarded as a manitou or god by the natives. It "must be highly esteemed by them," he wrote, "from the quantity of vermilion bestowed on it, and the number of animals depicted on the face of the rock." Many such drawings are to be seen on rocks in the border country even today. Few are so easy of access as the ones on Picture Rock in Crooked Lake.

On the canoe route from Grand Portage Norwood found at Moose Lake a wintering house of the Hudson's Bay Company. The steel engravings that accompany the printed report of this trip show a rugged country covered largely with coniferous trees, and made romantic with deep gorges and waterfalls.

In the 1860's and 1870's several other geologists explored the region. Most of them, like Newton H. Winchell, Henry H. Eames, Thomas Clark, and Robert Bell, have left printed records, from which we get the slight knowledge available for the period just before the area was opened to settlement.

Rumors of the extraordinary ore wealth of the region began in the French period and persisted down into the second half of the nineteenth century. Gold, copper, and iron were all mentioned. In 1864 Thomas Clark made a survey at state expense along a portion of the north shore of Lake Superior. The following year the state appropriated more money and Henry H. Eames continued the search, during which he penetrated to Vermilion Lake, found iron ore, and let it be known unofficially that he had found gold. Tremendous excitement followed. Some of the best-known persons in the young state's political and business life organized companies, such as the Mutual Protection Gold Miners Company of Minnesota, the Vermillion Falls Gold Mining Company, and the Minnesota Gold Mining Company, of which Henry H. Sibley was president. Roads were cleared, a sawmill was erected, and houses were built on the shore of Vermilion Lake. By 1866 the fastness of northern Minnesota's wilderness presented the odd sight of a typical mining camp on the shores of the great lake, with shafts sunk into quartz veins and mining works constructed near by. Three stamp mills were erected. The town site of Winston was laid out and shacks were built on it. Saloons and the other ordinary appurtenances of a mining village sprang up. Then the bubble was pricked. No gold was found. The mining companies disbanded, the miners departed, the shafts fell into disrepair. When private parties re-examined the region for gold in 1880, the competent expert whom they hired reported, "Not a trace of gold was discovered."

And all the while the most abundant bodies of commercially valuable iron ore in the world lay beneath the feet of the men trekking painfully through the forests of the mythical El Dorado. Later the lumbermen of the same area could not see the lasting commercial value of standing forests "because of the trees," and it took virtually complete deforestation to make people realize the tremendous economic value of a pine-covered vacation land.

Nearly twenty years passed after the Vermilion gold rush before the Vermilion Range shipped its first carload of iron ore. On July 31, 1884, a half holiday was declared at Soudan and the first trainload of ore was started off to Two Harbors. Between 1865 and 1884 George C. Stone of Duluth had convinced Charlemagne Tower, an eastern attorney for mining interests, of the presence of marketable ore on the Vermilion Range. Two surveys had been made, one by private interests in 1880 and the other by the state of Minnesota in 1878. Both proclaimed the presence of valuable ore in northeastern Minnesota. Still no action was taken till, late in 1882, the Minnesota Iron Company was incorporated. The town site of Tower was platted and laid out the same year. A charter was secured for the Duluth and Iron Range Railroad by the Minnesota Iron Company and by midsummer of 1884 a railroad had been constructed from Two Harbors to the range. In 1887 a veritable mining boom was unmistakable. By 1891 some 284 mining and quarrying companies had been incorporated under the laws of Minnesota. Ely was platted in 1887. It is the site of the great Chandler Mine. At most of the mines the *modus operandi* is the time-known way of getting hard ore out of deep veins, that is, by shaft and tunnel mining.

No one had ever heard in these parts of soft ore that lay, granule upon granule, as deposited by microscopic creatures in oceanic waters aeons ago, when northeastern Minnesota was coming into being geologically. Unlike the ore laid down on the Vermilion Range, it remained in a horizontal position on the Mesabi Range to the south. No folding of the earth's surface tilted the strata to a more vertical position. So ground waters did an incalculable service for man by leaching out the silica and leaving the ore in neat pockets or troughs, from which it could be taken by the unbelievably simple expedient of steam and electric scoops.[1] It was all so simple and cheap that it took great courage for the Merritt brothers of Duluth to believe and to proclaim that the red earth they had found on the Mesabi Range in 1890 was iron ore. Courage they had, however, and Mountain Iron Mine, four miles west of the present city of Virginia, was discovered and opened. Then the Biwabik Mine was opened, the first ore was shipped from it in 1892, railroads were built, and a great and frenzied boom set in. Soon Minnesota was producing more than half the country's annual supply of iron ore.

[1] It is said that the idea of using steam shovels to dig the Panama Canal came from the Mesabi Range.

From Finland and Jugoslavia

The range towns have developed personalities of their own, differing in many respects from other places in Minnesota or elsewhere. Great steel corporations with their subsidiaries soon had control of both mines and railroads, raising questions of labor, the laborer's rights, taxation, and so forth. Racial stocks not to be found in any numbers elsewhere in Minnesota became common on the ranges – Slovenians, Croatians, Serbians, Montenegrins, Bulgarians, and Italians; many Finns; and others. These men and their descendants have adapted themselves almost perfectly to the region and are now completely at home on the shores of the lakes of the North Country.

The Finns in particular have imprinted their customs on the region. No establishment of any size but has its *sauna*, or Finn bathhouse. A stove, formerly a cone-shaped stone fireplace, covered with small rocks is heated in the bathing room of the little, two-roomed house; water is thrown on the rocks; and in the resulting heat, from 150 to 165 degrees, the bather gets an invigorating, cleansing bath in invisible steam. Cold water thrown on the body completes the bath, unless one can jump into a near-by lake or stream or roll in snow and so obtain the desired reaction.

The *sauna* is more than an agency for cleanliness among the Finns. It is a social institution of fundamental importance as well. It is the first building erected by a Finn on his land. In it gather the neighbors, making their bath an opportunity for chatting and getting acquainted. About it still cluster some of the many charms and spells of a race that found in Minnesota's pine woods "the little people" of Finland's dark forests. A Finn who does not speak in his *sauna* on Shrove Tuesday may escape the bites of mosquitoes the following summer. A lad can learn the direction from which his sweetheart will come by observing the way his cedar or birch bath switch, or *vasta,* points after he has thrown it through his legs in the *sauna.*

Little farms on the edge of mining towns became the rule among the Finnish miners, who found winter unemployment a great drain on meager summer earnings in the mines. Soon the idea spread to other nationalities among the miners. Labor difficulties also helped the movement to spread, especially after the strike of 1907. It was after that year that Finnish farms became typical of the northern Minnesota landscape. A log *sauna,* hay barns sloping inward toward their foundations, odd gumdrop-shaped haystacks, and many outbuildings of one sort or another, carved post tops, and arrangements for carrying hay on two stretchers – all proclaim the owner of a northern farm to be a Finn, especially if the buildings are red and nestle under a hill on the edge of a solitary lake.

On those little farms one sees the sacred tree of Finnish legend, the mountain ash, called the "rowan tree" in Scotch lore. One of the many Finnish folk songs still sung on the range and elsewhere in Finnish communities is almost the duplicate of the plaintive Scotch ballad, "Edward," so appealing to all of us in our childhood. Miss Marjorie Edgar, who has collected many of the Finnish folk songs in Minnesota, has translated one of its twenty stanzas thus:

Why is your sword so red with blood,
O my gallant son?
I stabbed my brother, he is dead,
Mother, dearest mother.

Miss Edgar has also collected the old Finnish magic charms along the border waters. One that she found at Winton was to keep cold away, not a bad idea in border-land winters. It runs like this in Miss Edgar's translation:

Cold, thou son of Wind,
Do not freeze my finger nails,
Do not freeze my hands.
Freeze thou the water willows,
Go chill the birch chunks.

The purpose of most of these charms was, of course, to suggest another way for the evil to take. So, it was advised to betake itself elsewhere, sometimes even to one's acquaintances! Thus, a charm to get rid of hiccups suggested that they go to the loom, the bark, the birch, the needle, the thicket, the spruce, and, finally, to the neighbors. This ancient piece of folklore also was picked up at Winton.

One still hears on the border the "Kalevala," the epic of old Finland, the poem that inspired "Hiawatha," as the following excerpt reveals:

Then the aged Väinämöinen
Spoke aloud his songs of magic,
And a flower-crowned birch grew upward,
Crowned with flowers, and leaves all golden,
And its summit reached to heaven,
To the very clouds uprising.
Then he sang his songs of magic,
And he sang a moon all shining,
Sang the moon to shine forever
In the pine-tree's emerald summit,
Sang the Great Bear in its branches.

Longfellow went to northern Minnesota forests for Hiawatha the man, and to the "Kalevala" for the form of the poem.

By 1940 the population of northeastern Minnesota included a very large number of Slovenians and Croatians. A Slovenian scholar[1] deeply versed in Slovenian family names has made a study of the draft registraton list of October, 1940, at Ely, and reports that, of the young men between twenty-one and thirty-five registered at Ely for the district round about, practically a third had Slovenian names. Of the more than eighteen hundred names, over five hundred and forty were recognizable as Slovenian and fifty as Croatian. How many Americanized names are not recognizable it is impossible to say, but there are many.

These South Europeans began to have an interest in Minnesota about 1890, largely through their knowledge of three early missionaries to the Lake Superior Chippewa. Since 1835 the names of Friedrich Baraga, Franz Pierz, and Otto Skolla had been household words in the Austrian provinces of Carniola, Styria, and Illyria, as well as in southeastern Europe in general. Baraga was the leader, a man of princely family in Illyria, and of vast erudition, who responded to a Catholic bishop's pleading for his "red children" and came to the Lake Superior field in 1831. He spent the remainder of a long life there, preaching, teaching, making the best-known Chippewa dictionary and grammar, and publishing accounts of his work in European Catholic periodicals. Thus he attracted two other Slovenians, Pierz and Skolla, to his field. These men likewise published sketches of their countryside in America and its natives, which percolated to thousands of humble homes. Old Minnesota Slovenians remember the appeals of their old-country parish priests for contributions to the missions of

[1] His Americanized name is John Jager and he is a resident of Minneapolis.

Northern Winter

Northern Summer, Basswood Lake

Baraga, Pierz, Skolla, and their Slovenian successors. So, when the mines of Ely, Soudan, Tower, Chisholm, and other places were opened, the Slovenians already knew of Minnesota and came by scores to labor and eventually to live there. The similarity of the terrain and the climate to those of their native land made the region doubly appealing to them.

Canoeists on the border lakes often inquire why it is that the best guides are so frequently "Austrian" – referring to the Slovenians and Croatians, who remained Austrians till Jugoslavia separated from Austria at the close of the first World War. Louis Adamic, in his *My America*, gives an answer. Feudalism persisted in southeastern Europe till the twentieth century, and one of its manifestations was the restriction on hunting and fishing imposed by the overlords. Only they themselves had the privilege of carrying on those activities. The common man could not indulge his taste for shooting, hunting, and fishing. Once in the Minnesota wilds, however, he found all these pursuits open alike to rich and poor. So he did what he had long wanted to do – he took to the forest. There he became versed in wilderness ways and naturally put his new skills to commercial use.

Logging Days

JUST as our century opened, another chapter in the borderland's history was beginning. White and Norway pines constituted a large part of the coniferous area of northeastern Minnesota. These trees were now cut and sent to market, as the same species had been cut and marketed in New England, Michigan, Wisconsin, and southern Minnesota. First the trees in the triangle between the St. Croix and the Mississippi had been cut; then the stands on Rum, Snake, Kettle, Willow, and other rivers; and about 1880 lumber camps were found as far north as Pokegama Falls and neighboring points. In the nineties the Leech Lake and Itasca camps and mills were in full swing. And then the attack began on the last stand, along the lakes and streams of the border. Trees that had seen De Noyon's canoe on the lakes beneath their boughs came crashing down. Two hundred years of growth ended in a fourth as many minutes. Winton was founded in 1901, a lumber town of the first water. Virginia boasted the largest white pine sawmill in the world in 1900. Ely's streets and saloons – dozens of the latter – resounded with the clatter of calked boots on wood every spring after the drive was over. The saloonkeepers put new floors in their establishments every little while rather than lose the trade of woodsmen by complaining that their spiked shoes ruined wooden floors. The men came down from the drive with pockets full of the wages of an entire season. A few nights in the saloons and they were picked clean, all ready for another hard season in the woods.

Some profess to find romance in lumber camps. At least life there was simple, full of hard work and danger, with no dissipation, and with adequate though hardly ample menus, ruthless exploitation by most employers, destruction of game, some little fun, and a satisfying contact with Nature in some of her grandest moods.

The camps were great log cabins, where men slept in bunks, ate in silence at long, high tables, and played cards, whittled, or yarned of an evening, though sleep usually came early after long hours of labor in cold, bracing air. "Daylight in the swamp" sounded too early at best, even for men who had gone to bed with the birds. Baked beans, meat, bread, potatoes, some canned fruit, the ordinary vegetables, pancakes, doughnuts, pies, and cakes – these were the standard dishes, and might appear as well on the breakfast as on the dinner table. Lunch was eaten in the woods on logs and stumps, having been brought there by the cookee in the "swing-dingle."

Many horses were used for pulling the great bobsleds of logs along iced ruts. Fine teams were the rule. The complaint was often made that the horses received better attention than the men. Toward the end of the logging period, a brand-new contraption was used, a "steam hauler," which laid its own track, the ancestor of the modern caterpillar tractor.

Lumberjacks had their own costume, their own vocabulary, their own songs. It is even said that they had their own Paul Bunyan yarns, but the proof of that statement has yet to appear. Most of the old woodsmen of reliable memory disclaim any knowledge of Paul or his blue ox. It is noticeable that a large percentage of the songs in Rickaby's *Songs of the Shanty-Boy* were sung for the compiler by Minnesota lumberjacks.

One of the most commonly sung ditties in border-lakes camps was "Gerry's Rocks."

GERRY'S ROCKS[1]

Come all ye true born shanty-boys, whoever that ye be,
I would have you pay attention and listen unto me,
Concerning a young shanty-boy, so tall, genteel, and brave.
'T was on a jam on Gerry's Rocks he met a wat'ry grave.

It happened on a Sunday morn as you shall quickly hear.
Our logs were piled up mountain high, there being no one to keep
them clear.

[1] From Franz Rickaby, *Ballads and Songs of the Shanty-Boy* (Cambridge, 1926), reprinted by permission of the President and Fellows of Harvard College.

Our boss he cried, "Turn out, brave boys. Your hearts are void of fear.
We'll break that jam on Gerry's Rocks, and for Agonstown we'll steer."

Some of them were willing enough, but others they hung back.
'T was for to work on Sabbath they did not think 't was right.
But six of our brave Canadian boys did volunteer to go
And break the jam on Gerry's Rocks with their foreman, young Monroe.

They had not rolled off many logs when the boss to them did say,
"I'd have you be on your guard, brave boys. That jam will soon give way."
But scarce the warning had he spoke when the jam did break and go,
And it carried away these six brave youths and their foreman, young Monroe.

When the rest of the shanty-boys these sad tidings came to hear,
To search for their dead comrades to the river they did steer.
One of these a headless body found, to their sad grief and woe,
Lay cut and mangled on the beach the head of young Monroe.

They took him from the water and smoothed down his raven hair.
There was one fair form amongst them, her cries would rend the air.
There was one fair form amongst them, a maid from Saginaw town.
Her sighs and cries would rend the skies for her lover that was drowned.

They buried him quite decently, being on the seventh of May,
Come all the rest of you shanty-boys, for your dead comrade pray.
'T is engraved on a little hemlock tree that at his head doth grow,
The name, the date, and the drowning of this hero, young Monroe.

Miss Clara was a noble girl, likewise the raftsman's friend.
Her mother was a widow woman lived at the river's bend.
The wages of her own true love the boss to her did pay,
And a liberal subscription she received from the shanty-boys next
day.

Miss Clara did not long survive her great misery and grief.
In less than three months afterwards death came to her relief.
In less than three months afterwards she was called to go,
And her last request was granted – to be laid by young Monroe.

Come all the rest of ye shanty-men who would like to go and
see,
On a little mound by the river's bank there stands a hemlock tree.
The shanty-boys cut the woods all round. These lovers they lie
low.
Here lies Miss Clara Dennison and her shanty-boy, Monroe.

In the bunkhouses of the North Country slept men of many nationalities. In this respect the Basswood, Kawishiwi, and "Range" camps of the late 1890's and early 1900's differed from those of an earlier period. In the New England, Michigan, Wisconsin, and more southerly Minnesota camps, the men were mostly Yankees, with some slight admixture of Canadians, "Canucks," and even some Scandinavians. By the 1890's, however, their roles were being played increasingly in Minnesota by Swedes, Finns, and South Europeans. In the twentieth century the predominance of non-English stock was striking.

A change took place also in logging methods early in the century. Railroads began to reach into obscure corners of the area; Russell cars shipped the logs straight from skidways to distant mills without reloading; McGiffert loaders replaced the top and bottom loaders, or jammers, at the skidways; and there were other innovations. But there was romance even in machinery. Who can look at a Shay locomotive even today and not feel the corners of his mouth twist a little? It brings to mind the funny little railroads that spread out into Minnesota's northlands, laid nonchalantly over hill and dale, around corners, into camps and out, with scarcely a thought of grading. One encounters them at the most unexpected places even today — that is, traces of them, for even as this is written their day, too, is ending and their rails are being taken up to help spread ruin and disaster in the wars of Europe and Asia. In their place has come the truck. Only one stationary mill, at Virginia, operates today. Portable mills now cut the logs brought in by the trucks of individuals.

Recent History

THE BORDER COUNTRY's recent history may be said to have begun in one sense in 1909 with the passage of an act of Congress creating the Superior National Forest. Simultaneously the Quetico Provincial Park was created on the opposite shores by the province of Ontario. Too much praise can hardly be given to the individuals and governments that were responsible for this far-visioned action. The period of despoiling was approaching its end and the era of conservation was beginning. The Superior National Forest is one of the largest forests in the United States, stretching along the border line some 180 miles westward from Lake Superior. It contains almost three million acres, of which nearly a fifth is water surface. There are over fifteen hundred lakes in the forest. Parts of the forest are designated game refuges.

Federal forest officers and rangers protect and administer the forest. Many lookout towers of steel, ninety feet high, have been placed in strategic places. From them keen eyes watch constantly for forest fires, the scourge of the North Country. CCC camps in recent years have been of great usefulness in the forest. Their men have cleaned out slashings left from logging operations, windfalls, and other fire hazards; eradicated ribes, the alternate host of the white pine blister rust; cut portages and marked them; built canoe landings; and constructed camp sites.

A Logging Scene on Stony River near Ely, about 1910

Cook Shanty of a Logging Camp near Ely, about 1910

An Old Logging Trestle on Fall Lake

Campfire on a Northern Lake

All this has not been secured without a fight. About 1925 private power and pulp companies, by attempting to construct dams, were threatening the continuance of the border-lakes region as the last great wilderness and canoeing country in the United States. An aroused public, finally aware of what was going on, created an international body, the Quetico-Superior Council with headquarters in Minneapolis, to serve as a clearinghouse for individuals and organizations in Canada and the United States in protecting the North Country. Shortly the council secured the enactment of legislation by Congress and the Minnesota legislature designating a wilderness area in northeastern Minnesota which Congress proposed to protect. It embraces the country south and east of Rainy Lake as far as North Lake just east of Gunflint Lake. Baleful projects in the area have frequently been thwarted.

The council's main objects at present are: acquisition by the Federal government of lands privately owned in the designated area; and a treaty with Canada assuring co-operative administration of the twin areas by both countries in such a manner that their value as a great public recreation ground, canoe country, and wild-life sanctuary will not be unnecessarily interfered with by the utilization of its other public values. A truly adequate program cannot be maintained until much of the area within the United States has become public property. No long-range planning can be undertaken until it is certain that the Canadian part of the area is to be maintained in the same spirit and with the same objectives as the part south of the line. Dominion as well as provincial action and control are therefore necessary. The International Joint Commission is a great factor in furthering this enterprise, but the Dominion can do little till it has reached an agreement with the province of Ontario. Then a treaty between Canada and the United States can be made. Anticipatory of such a treaty, an agreement concerning water-level matters on the boundary was ratified by the two countries in 1940. The list of men and women of both countries who are on record as favoring the purposes and objectives of the council reads like the pages of *Who's Who.*

In 1934 the President of the United States created the Quetico-Superior Committee as an advisory agency to further the program of protection and promotion in the twin areas.

Why do great nations, famous men, artists, writers, sportsmen, and many others go to such lengths to establish a wilderness area in Minnesota and Ontario? What does it offer that is so unique? What can one expect to find there? What is its siren song that lures men and women thither year after year in increasing numbers?

Every one of them would answer in a slightly different way, if the question were put. One would remark that he is interested in the fishing; another that he goes to the north woods to see magnificent white and Norway pines; another that he hopes to see moose there; a fourth that he finds the canoe trips unexcelled. So the answers would run. One man's reply was something like this: "No matter how many answers you obtain from different people, you will find there are certain common denominators: simplicity – solitude – nature, untouched by man – mental, physical, spiritual rejuvenation. These are the factors which either characterize man's longing for this country or are necessary for the particular enjoyment which he desires. Man has a right to solitude and simplicity. It should be one of the few inalienable rights. They are the essential elements of religion, philosophy, of all exaltation of the spirit. But how obtain it on a continent rapidly becoming crowded and covered with man's handiwork? Solely by retaining areas still unspoiled, large enough to give every man his mile, near enough to urban centers to permit the ordinary man to get there in an ordinary way. Once despoiled or defiled, these areas are gone – for a geological age."

These appeals have already been mentioned: the unusual geology, the memories of intrepid explorers, the echoes of voyageurs' songs, the French names of the portages, the Indian wigwam on the shore, the joy of plunging through white water in a canoe, the "Come-all-ya's," or lumberjacks' chantey's, the search for a trading post site of a hundred years ago. There are still other appeals.

As you wander through the woods in July, you will find the twinflower. Its evergreen vines alone might be overlooked, but that anyone should miss it in bloom is unthinkable. Its exquisite markings, its tiny twin bells, and its perfume, so heavy for so frail a thing, all shout its perfection to you. It bears the name of the great eighteenth-century Swedish botanist, Linnaeus, the founder of modern systematic botany, and is called scientifically *Linnaea*. It is said that Linnaeus discovered it on a trip to Finland and ever after considered it his favorite flower. Other plants and flowers that bring fond memories to Scandinavians are the saxifrage, the bellwort, the foamflower, the clintonia, and many more. These and the stemless lady's-slipper, the partridge berry, the shinleaf, the bunchberry, the arbutus, the fringed gentian, the fringed polygala, and the pitcher plant will bring nostalgic joy to New Englanders. True Minnesotans will always cherish the magnificent showy moccasin flowers, which can seldom be found now except in the north woods. The region is a paradise for lovers of plants and flowers, from April to November.

Bird lovers are no less enthusiastic about it. Even today the gray-blue spruce grouse may be seen in the tamarack and spruce forests about Ely. Black ducks – "black mallards" in local parlance – are extending into the region from the East and fly past you on the larger lakes, giving you a fleeting glimpse of the silver linings of their swift wings. The duck with reddish head and a little crest seen at the waterfalls, leading little balls of down that climb all over its back, is the female American merganser. The large whitish bird resembling a loon that accompanies her early in the summer is the male. Mergansers fly when you approach, but the scores of loons that you will encounter in any day's voyage on a large lake will invariably dive, leaving no trace of their departure except the haunting echoes of their cries. On one of the islands of the "English Channel" of Basswood Lake you will see the heronries, where tall blue herons stand stork-like at the edge of broken-twig nests in the tops of gaunt trees. Partridges nest trustingly near cabins in May, cluck to downy broods in summer, and come to feeding boards all winter. Whisky jacks – "lumberjacks" to residents of the region – will share everything on your table with you, with the one exception of raw onions. Nor will these Canada jays be bashful and wait till you have finished or they are invited.

There are birds of special interest – the American and the Arctic three-toed woodpeckers, the Hudsonian chickadee, the blue-headed vireo, the parula warbler, the crossbills, the Connecticut and the mourning warblers, and the many scarlet tanagers. The sight of an osprey plunging into the lake in a wild spray of spreading water as he catches a fish; the gangster antics of a bald eagle seizing the fish from the osprey; the long joyous burst of a winter wren's paean; the maniac laughter of loons; the drumming of partridges from all about the lake in the mating season – any or all of these may reward the quick of sight and ear.

And then, in the hush of the forest, perhaps while you are toiling along some portage path, you will hear from a distant thicket a hymn never meant for mortal ears. No trace of earth in the hermit thrush's sublime matins and vespers – only the ecstasy of serene faith.

Chronology

Before Recorded History[1]

500,000,000 B.C.	The northeastern Minnesota country emerges.
350,000,000 B.C.	The Saganaga Lake granites are formed.
200,000,000 B.C.	The Mesabi iron ore is deposited; the volcanic rocks of the north shore of Lake Superior are laid down.
25,000,000 B.C.	Dinosaurs come and go.
500,000 B.C. TO HISTORIC TIMES	The ice age comes and passes in four stages, ending with the formation and gradual disappearance of Lake Agassiz; the age of elephants comes and passes; early man appears; coniferous forests move north and are followed by deciduous forests; the Rainy River country is inhabited by mound builders.

Recorded History

1500 A.D.	By this time the northeastern Minnesota country is occupied by Sioux Indians.
1609	Virginia Colony is given a charter, by which she claims the northeastern Minnesota country as part of her territory.
1659–60	The first white men, Radisson and Des Groseilliers, visit the region.
1660	The Chippewa Indians begin to push out the Sioux.
1670	The Hudson's Bay Company is organized in London.

[1] Dates in this chronology are perforce approximate in several instances.

The French Flag

1671	The northeastern Minnesota country is formally annexed to France in a ceremony held at Sault Ste. Marie by St. Lusson, who claims for France all interior North America.
1679–80	Du Lhut explores the region.
1689	De Noyon explores the canoe route west from Lake Superior and Rainy Lake.
1731	La Vérendrye and his relatives explore the canoe route and build a fort on Rainy River.
1732	La Vérendrye establishes Fort St. Charles on Lake of the Woods.
1732–56	Many French traders and explorers pass over the canoe route.
1736	Bourassa builds a fort on Little Vermilion Lake.
1760	The first English traders invade the Lake Superior country.

The British Flag

1763	Northeastern Minnesota becomes British by the Treaty of Paris between Great Britain and France.
1767	Jonathan Carver visits the Grand Portage end of the canoe route.
1768	John Askin clears the site of Grand Portage village and builds a fort.

Province of Quebec

1774	Northeastern Minnesota becomes a part of the province of Quebec under the Quebec Act, although the region is still claimed by Virginia under her charter of 1609.
1775	Peter Pond and Alexander Henry, the Elder, first use the canoe route.
1778	The North West Company is organized; the presence of British soldiers at Grand Portage brings the region into the Revolutionary War.
1783	By treaty with the United States, Great Britain gives up the border-lakes country on paper, but actually retains it till the end of the War of 1812, making several

attempts to change the boundary line; Virginia relinquishes her claim to the northeastern Minnesota country.

NORTHWEST TERRITORY

1787 The Northwest Territory, including northeastern Minnesota, is established; the Ordinance of 1787 gives the region a constitution and government under the United States.

1789 Alexander Mackenzie uses the border canoe route on the journey resulting in the discovery of the Mackenzie River.

1793 Mackenzie again passes over the route on his way to the Pacific, and John Macdonell also uses it; the Hudson's Bay Company establishes a post at the outlet of Rainy Lake, its first in the region; the border-lakes route has now become the great highway to the beaver country, with hundreds of traders passing over it annually.

1797 David Thompson joins the North West Company and visits the region.

INDIANA TERRITORY

1800 Northeastern Minnesota becomes part of Indiana Territory; Alexander Henry, the Younger, uses the canoe route.

1804 Grand Portage is abandoned in favor of Fort William; the Kaministikwia route replaces the border-lakes canoe route.

The British and American Flags

1806 Lieutenant Zebulon M. Pike of the United States Army raises the American flag over the northeastern Minnesota region.

1808 John Jacob Astor incorporates the American Fur Company.

ILLINOIS TERRITORY

1809 Northeastern Minnesota becomes part of Illinois Territory.

1812 Lord Selkirk establishes the Red River settlement.

1816 Congress prohibits foreigners from engaging in the fur trade on American soil, thus enabling Astor to get control of the fur trade of northeastern Minnesota.

The American Flag

MICHIGAN TERRITORY

1818 Northeastern Minnesota becomes part of Michigan Territory.

1821 The North West and Hudson's Bay companies unite.

1822–24 British and American boundary commissioners explore the border canoe routes to determine upon an international boundary line.

1833–47 The Hudson's Bay and American Fur companies agree to eliminate competition in the boundary region.

WISCONSIN TERRITORY

1836 Northeastern Minnesota becomes part of Wisconsin Territory.

1842 The American Fur Company fails.

1848 Wisconsin becomes a state, leaving the Minnesota country without organized government.

MINNESOTA TERRITORY

1849 The region becomes part of Minnesota Territory; David Dale Owen's geological survey explores northeastern Minnesota.

1857 Hind and Dawson explore the "Dawson Trail."

STATE OF MINNESOTA

1858 The region becomes part of the state of Minnesota.

1865 The Vermilion Lake gold rush begins.

1884 The first iron ore is shipped from the Vermilion Range.

1890 Iron is discovered on the Mesabi Range; lumbering begins in northeastern Minnesota.

1909 The Superior National Forest is created; the United States and Canada establish the International Joint Commission.

1934 The Quetico-Superior Committee is appointed.

Bibliography

Printed Works[1]

ADAMIC, LOUIS. From Many Lands. New York and London, Harper & Brothers, [1940].

——— My America, 1928–1938. New York and London, Harper & Brothers, 1938.

ANDREWS, CHRISTOPHER C. Christopher C. Andrews, Pioneer in Forestry Conservation in the United States. . . . Edited by his daughter, Alice E. Andrews, with an introduction by William Watts Folwell. Cleveland, The Arthur H. Clark Company, 1928.

BARBEAU, CHARLES MARIUS, and EDWARD SAPIR. Folk Songs of French Canada. New Haven, Yale University Press, 1925.

BIGSBY, JOHN J. The Shoe and Canoe, or Pictures of Travel in the Canadas. . . . London, Chapman and Hall, 1850. 2 v. in 1.

BLEGEN, THEODORE C. Building Minnesota. Boston and New York, D. C. Heath and Company, [1938].

BUCK, SOLON J. The Story of Grand Portage. In Minnesota History Bulletin, v. 5, p. 14–27. February, 1923.

BURPEE, LAWRENCE J., editor. Journals and Letters of Pierre Gaultier de Varennes de La Vérendrye and His Sons. . . . Toronto, The Champlain Society, 1927.

——— The Search for the Western Sea: The Story of the Exploration of North-western America. Toronto, The Macmillan Company of Canada, limited, 1935.

CANADA. PROVINCIAL SECRETARY'S OFFICE. Papers Relative to

[1] This is a selected list of books and a few manuscripts which will assist readers to continue their study of the history of the border-lakes region of Minnesota. It makes no profession of being complete.

the Exploration of the Country between Lake Superior and the Red River Settlement. . . . London, Her Majesty's Stationery Office, 1859.

CLEMENTS, J. MORGAN. The Vermilion Iron-bearing District of Minnesota. (Department of the Interior. Monographs of the United States Geological Survey, v. 45. 57 Congress, 2 session. House Documents, 433). Washington, Government Printing Office, 1903.

COUES, ELLIOTT, editor. New Light on the Early History of the Greater Northwest: The Manuscript Journals of Alexander Henry . . . and of David Thompson . . . 1799–1814. . . . New York, Francis P. Harper, 1897. 3 v.

DAVIDSON, GORDON C. The North West Company. Berkeley, University of California Press, 1918.

DAWSON, SIMON J. See CANADA. PROVINCIAL SECRETARY'S OFFICE.

DENSMORE, FRANCES. Chippewa Customs. (Smithsonian Institution. Bureau of American Ethnology. Bulletin 86). Washington, Government Printing Office, 1929.

——— Chippewa Music. (Smithsonian Institution. Bureau of American Ethnology. Bulletin 45). Washington, Government Printing Office, 1910.

——— Chippewa Music — II. (Smithsonian Institution. Bureau of American Ethnology. Bulletin 53). Washington, Government Printing Office, 1913.

DE KRUIF, PAUL H. Seven Iron Men. New York, Harcourt, Brace and Company, [1929].

EDGAR, MARJORIE. Finnish Charms and Folk Songs in Minnesota. In Minnesota History, v. 17, p. 406–410. December, 1936.

FEDERAL WRITERS' PROJECT OF THE WORKS PROGRESS ADMINISTRATION. Minnesota; a State Guide. (American Guide Series). New York, The Viking Press, 1938.

FOLWELL, WILLIAM W. A History of Minnesota. St. Paul, Minnesota Historical Society, 1921–30. 4 v.

FRANCHÈRE, GABRIEL. Narrative of a Voyage to the Northwest Coast of America in the Years 1811, 1812, 1813 and 1814. . . . Translated and edited by J. V. Huntington. New York, Redfield, 1854.

GATES, CHARLES M., editor. Five Fur Traders of the Northwest; Being the Narrative of Peter Pond and the Diaries of John Macdonell, Archibald N. McLeod, Hugh Faries, and Thomas Connor. With an introduction by Grace Lee Nute. Published for the Minnesota Society of Colonial Dames of America. Minneapolis, The University of Minnesota Press, 1933.

GIBBON, JOHN MURRAY, editor and translator. Canadian Folk Songs (Old and New). Harmonizations by Geoffrey O'Hara and Oscar O'Brien. New York, E. P. Dutton & Co., 1927.

HALL, SHERMAN. Reminiscences of Missionary Life in the Northwest, No. 7. In The New Era. Sauk Rapids, Minnesota, June 28, 1860.

HARMON, DANIEL W. A Journal of Voyages and Travels in the Interior of North America, between the 47th and 58th Degrees of North Latitude, Extending from Montreal nearly to the Pacific, a Distance of about 5,000 Miles. . . . Toronto, The Courier Press, 1911.

HENRY, ALEXANDER. Travels & Adventures in Canada and the Indian Territories between the Years 1760 and 1776. Edited by James Bain. Boston, Little, Brown & Company, 1901.

HENRY, ALEXANDER. See COUES, ELLIOTT, editor.

HIND, HENRY Y. Narrative of the Canadian Red River Exploring Expedition of 1857 and of the Assinniboine and Saskatchewan Exploring Expedition of 1858. London, Green, Longman and Roberts, 1860. 2 v.

——— Reports of Progress, together with a Preliminary Report, on the Assinniboine and Saskatchewan Exploring Expedition. . . . London, Her Majesty's Stationery Office, 1860.

——— See CANADA. PROVINCIAL SECRETARY'S OFFICE.

HOLBROOK, STEWART H. Holy Old Mackinaw; a Natural History of the American Lumberjack. New York, The Macmillan Company, 1938.

——— Iron Brew; a Century of American Ore and Steel. New York, The Macmillan Company, 1939.

INNIS, HAROLD A. The Fur Trade in Canada; an Introduction to Canadian Economic History. New Haven, Yale University Press, 1930.

INTERNATIONAL BOUNDARY COMMISSION. Joint Report upon the Survey and Demarcation of the Boundary between the United States and Canada, from the Northwesternmost Point of Lake of the Woods to Lake Superior. . . . Washington, Government Printing Office, 1931.

INTERNATIONAL JOINT COMMISSION. Final Report . . . on the Lake of the Woods Reference. Washington, Government Printing Office, 1917.

JENKS, ALBERT E. Recent Discoveries in Minnesota Prehistory. In Minnesota History, v. 16, p. 1–21. March, 1935.

KANE, PAUL. Wanderings of an Artist among the Indians of North America from Canada . . . through the Hudson's Bay Company's Territory. . . . Toronto, The Radisson Society of Canada, limited, 1925.

KELLOGG, LOUISE P. The British Régime in Wisconsin and the Northwest. Madison, State Historical Society of Wisconsin, 1935.

——The French Régime in Wisconsin and the Northwest. Madison, State Historical Society of Wisconsin, 1925.

LA VÉRENDRYE, PIERRE GAULTIER, SIEUR DE. See BURPEE, LAWRENCE J., editor.

MCKAY, DOUGLAS. The Honourable Company, a History of the Hudson's Bay Company. Indianapolis and New York, The Bobbs-Merrill Company, [1936].

MCKENNEY, THOMAS L. Sketches of a Tour to the Lakes, of the Character and Customs of the Chippewa Indians, and of Incidents Connected with the Treaty of Fond du Lac. . . . Baltimore, F. Lucas, jun'r., 1827.

MACKENZIE, ALEXANDER. Voyages from Montreal through the Continent of North America to the Frozen and Pacific Oceans in 1789 and 1793, with an Account of the Rise and State of the Fur Trade. New York, A. S. Barnes and Company, 1903.

NUTE, GRACE LEE. The Voyageur. New York and London, D. Appleton and Company, 1931.

OWEN, DAVID DALE. Report of a Geological Survey of Wisconsin, Iowa, and Minnesota. . . . Philadelphia, Lippincott, Gambro & Company, 1852.

POWELL, LOUIS H. Around a Geologic Clock in Minnesota. In Minnesota History, v. 15, p. 141–147. June, 1934.

RICKABY, FRANZ, collector and editor. Ballads and Songs of the Shanty-Boy. Cambridge, Harvard University Press, 1926.

ROBERTS, THOMAS S. The Birds of Minnesota. Minneapolis, The University of Minnesota Press, 1932. 2 v.

SEVAREID, ARNOLD E. Canoeing with the Cree. New York, The Macmillan Company, 1935.

SHEPHARD, ESTHER. Paul Bunyan. Seattle, The McNeil Press, [1924].

SHIRAS, GEORGE, 3D. Hunting Wild Life with Camera and Flashlight. A Record of Sixty-five Years' Visits to the Woods and Waters of North America. Washington, National Geographic Society, 1936.

STEVENS, JAMES. Paul Bunyan. New York, A. A. Knopf, 1925.

TANNER, JOHN. A Narrative of the Captivity and Adventures of John Tanner (U. S. Interpreter at the Saut de Ste. Marie) during Thirty Years Residence among the Indians in the Interior of North America. Edited by Edwin James. New York, C. & C. & H. Carvill, 1830.

THOMPSON, DAVID. See TYRRELL, J. B., editor.

——— See COUES, ELLIOTT, editor.

TYRRELL, J. B., editor. David Thompson's Narrative of His Explorations in Western America, 1784–1812. Toronto, The Champlain Society, 1916.

UNITED STATES CONGRESS. COMMITTEE ON PUBLIC LANDS. Superior National Forest Minnesota. Hearings before the Committee on the Public Lands Seventieth Congress First Session on H. R. 12780. . . . Washington, Government Printing Office, 1928.

WALLACE, W. STEWART, editor. Documents Relating to the North West Company. Toronto, The Champlain Society, 1934.

WARREN, WILLIAM W. History of the Ojibways, Based upon Traditions and Oral Statements. In Collections of the Minnesota Historical Society, v. 5, p. 21–394. St. Paul, Minnesota Historical Society, 1885.

WILLARD, DANIEL E. The Story of the North Star State. St. Paul, Webb Publishing Company, [1922].

WINCHELL, NEWTON H. The Aborigines of Minnesota. . . . St. Paul, The Minnesota Historical Society, 1911.

MANUSCRIPT SOURCES

HALL, SHERMAN. A letter by Hall to his brother, dated Lac du Flambeau, September 30, 1832, describing the methods of building construction used by the fur traders, is among Hall's papers, which are owned by Mr. Ernest W. Butterfield of Hartford, Connecticut. Photostatic copies of these papers are in the possession of the Minnesota Historical Society.

HUDSON'S BAY COMPANY ARCHIVES. Among the papers of this ancient corporation in London are many journals and reports of traders in the company's Lac La Pluie District, including those by Dr. John McLoughlin and J. D. Cameron in the 1820's, which were of particular value for this volume. These archives were used by the author with the kind permission of the Governor and Committee of the Hudson's Bay Company.

McLOUGHLIN, JOHN. Description of the Indians from Fort William to Lake of the Woods. This manuscript is owned by the library of McGill University, Montreal. A photostatic copy is in the possession of the Minnesota Historical Society. (See also HUDSON'S BAY COMPANY ARCHIVES).

THOMPSON, DAVID. Thompson's manuscript diaries, maps, and other records are in the possession of the Department of Public Records and Archives of the Province of Ontario at Toronto. Photostatic copies are owned by the Minnesota Historical Society. The diaries of 1797, 1798, and 1822 were of especial value for this book.

Index

Index

This book has been printed from Janson type for the Minnesota Historical Society

CROOKED LAKE
MOOSE BAY
KETT LAKE
PICTURE ROCKS
LAKE
CROOKED
LOWER BASSWOOD FALLS
WHEELBARROW PORTAGE
BASSWOOD RIVER
HORSE PORTAGE
BASSWOOD FALLS
BASSWOOD LAKE
RIVER
HORSE
LAKE
HORSE
JACKFISH BAY
PIPESTONE BAY
HOIST BAY
MI. PORTAGE

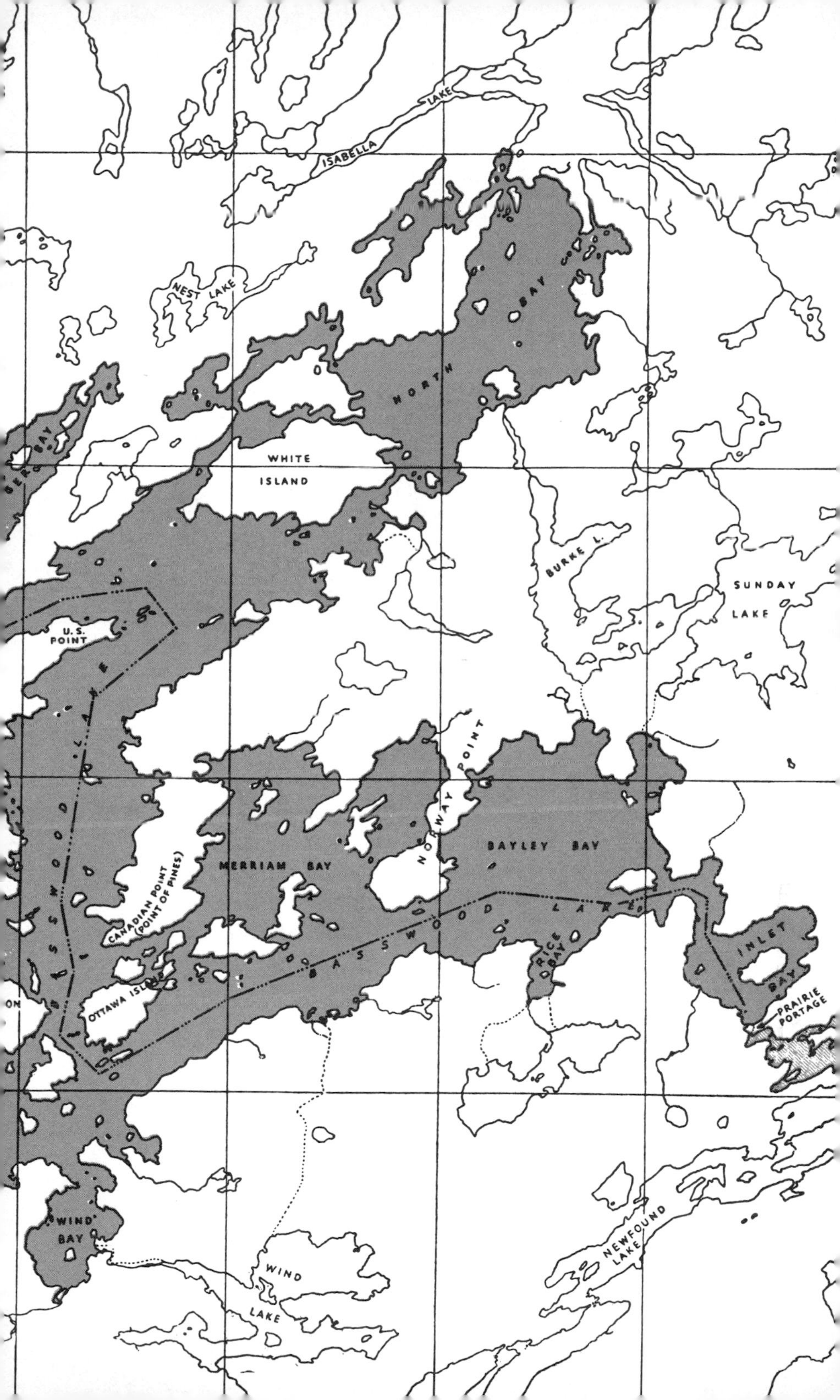
ISABELLA LAKE
NEST LAKE
NORTH BAY
WHITE ISLAND
BURKE L.
SUNDAY LAKE
U.S. POINT
NORWAY POINT
BAYLEY BAY
MERRIAM BAY
CANADIAN POINT (POINT OF PINES)
BASSWOOD LAKE
RICE BAY
INLET BAY
PRAIRIE PORTAGE
OTTAWA ISLAND
WIND BAY
WIND LAKE
NEWFOUND LAKE